BRODART
P9-DER-037

DISCARD

# THE ROMANS
## Life in the Empire

BY CHARLES GUITTARD

Illustrations by Annie-Claude Martin

Translated by Mary Kae LaRose

PEOPLES OF THE PAST

The Millbrook Press
Brookfield, Connecticut

Library of Congress Cataloging-in-Publication Data

Guittard, Charles.
[Autour de la Mediterranée, les Romains. English]
The Romans : life in the Empire / by Charles Guittard :
illustrated by Annie-Claude Martin : translated by Mary Kae LaRose.
p. cm.—(Peoples of the past)
Translation of: Autour de la Mediterranée, les Romains.
Includes bibliographical references (p. ) and index.
Summary: Discusses the formation of the Roman Empire, the daily
life of its inhabitants, and their accomplishments in the areas of
art, music, writing, and science.
ISBN 1-56294-200-X (lib.bdg.) ISBN 0-7613-0097-X (pbk.)
1. Rome—Social life and customs—Juvenile literature. [1. Rome—
Social life and customs.] I. Martin, Annie Claude, ill.
II. Title. III. Series: Peuples du passé. English.
DG78.G94 1992
937—dc20 92-9467 CIP AC

First published in the United States by
The Millbrook Press Inc.
2 Old New Milford Road, Brookfield, Connecticut 06804



Originally published as Autour de la Mediterranée,
les Romains (Peuples du passé series), Editions Nathan,
Paris


Printed in the United States of America

5 4 3 2

# CONTENTS

# INTRODUCTION

The Romans created one of the most magnificent and fascinating empires that the world has ever known. We have been able to reconstruct their civilization, in large part, because the Romans built things to last. The Roman Empire exists today in skeletal form. Buildings, bridges, roads, and aqueducts; sculptures, bas-reliefs, paintings, and mosaics; pottery, glass, and metal artifacts help us to draw a fairly accurate picture of who these people were.

In addition, scholars pour over the writings that the Romans left behind to learn about their discoveries, beliefs, opinions, and dreams. Latin, their official language, is the root of many European languages, including Italian, Spanish, and French. Roman law and principles of justice and tolerance are the basis for our laws today.

Some Roman customs and character traits are distasteful, though. Romans loved bloody spectacles, for instance. There are many stories about the decadence of wealthy Romans and their disdain for the less fortunate masses. And Romans were intolerant of a new religion based on worship of only one God—namely, Christianity.

The ancient Romans, like a well-known relative or friend, may upset us at times, but we are so firmly anchored to them that to cut adrift of our Roman heritage would mean the loss of our own identity.

Turn to the back of the book to get an idea of when the Roman Republic made way for the Empire and how long the Empire lasted. A map shows the lands conquered in the name of Rome, which by the time of the fall of the Western Roman Empire in A.D. 476 included about one fourth of Europe, the entire northern coast of Africa, and most of the Middle East.

This book hopes to bring the peoples of this giant empire to life so that you will know them: how they dressed, what they liked to eat and read and think about, what they meant to say with their lives.

# THE FORMATION OF THE EMPIRE

According to legend, the city of Rome was founded by the twins Romulus and Remus, sons of the war god Mars. Abandoned as infants on the bank of the Tiber River, they were nursed by a she-wolf until some shepherds rescued them. The boys grew up in the hills overlooking the river. One day, Romulus killed his brother Remus in a violent quarrel. He then founded the city that bears his name.

Even though the earliest days of Rome are shrouded in mystery, evidence does exist of a community on this site in the eighth century B.C., probably in 753. Over the following 1,300 years, Rome gradually took over the Italian peninsula, expanded into the lands surrounding the Mediterranean Sea, and grew into a tremendous empire stretching from the British Isles to North Africa, and from Spain to the Persian Gulf. By the fall of Rome in A.D. 476 this vast civilization had laid the groundwork—the language and literature, the judicial and political principles, the architecture, the theories about science, painting, and philosophy—for the Western world to come.

It took more than seven hundred years for Rome to establish its empire. Until 509 B.C., Rome was governed by kings. But the people rebelled and set up a republic. A group of men called the Senate made most of the decisions in the Republic. They handled the financial and foreign policies, and they passed the official orders that ruled the behavior of the rest of the citizens, or *plebians*. Two consuls were elected each year from the Senate to head the government.

Rome prospered in the Republic. The Romans faced tough mountain warriors called Samnites in central Italy. They stood up against many invasions by the Gauls and Etruscans, who swept down through

the mountains of northern Italy. To the south of Rome, Greek colonists lived in the bustling cities of Naples, Taranto, Herculaneum, Crotone, and Sybaris. But in 272 B.C., Taranto fell, and soon after that, all of southern Italy came under Roman domination. By 265 B.C. the Romans had also established themselves firmly in the north. The most bitter enemy of all, though, remained: the Carthaginians. For over a century, fierce wars raged between Rome and the North African empire of Carthage. Finally, in 146 B.C. Roman troops under the leadership of Scipio Aemilianus seized and destroyed Carthage. Rome became the greatest Mediterranean power.

**Julius Caesar**

*Born in 100 or 101 B.C., Caesar became a consul in 59 B.C. He left to govern Cisalpine Gaul, the southeastern region of present-day France. From there, he launched a campaign to conquer all of Gaul. The Gallic War (58–51 B.C.) ended with the defeat of Vercingetorix, the supreme commander of the Gauls. In 46 B.C. Caesar was named dictator and consul for ten years. During this time he tried to replace the Republic with a monarchy. But he was assassinated on March 15, 44 B.C. It was his heir Octavius who realized Caesar's ambition when he became the first emperor of Rome.*

Soon after this victory, though, the Republic was torn apart by the chaos of civil war. Octavius, Julius Caesar's adopted son, brought peace to the warring Republic and established a centralized form of government called *princeps senatus,* in which all power was in the hands of a single ruler. In 27 B.C. Octavius—later called Augustus—became the first in a long line of Roman emperors. Under his rule, the Roman Empire was born.

## ROMAN CONQUERORS

The Romans were not the first people to build an empire. The Greeks, Carthaginians, and Phoenicians had extended their influence by founding colonies in foreign lands. Most of these settlements were located at important seaports; they brought in additional resources and secured trade routes. But they remained outposts.

The Romans were different. When they looked beyond their own territory, they sought to conquer rather than to live alongside the people who had already claimed the land. Power meant taking over new territory regardless of what wealth or strategic location the new place offered them. It was the Roman legion that made these conquests possible. In the first century B.C., Roman legions were bodies of six thousand men divided into ten troops, or cohorts, of six hundred each. A troop was itself divided into smaller groups called maniples. These were split into units of one hundred men called centuries. Each legion had a number, a name such as Augusta or Gallica, and a nickname.

By the second century A.D., Rome had roughly thirty legions. In addition to its foot soldiers, each legion had as many as three hundred cavalrymen. Auxiliary regiments were made up of noncitizen troops from lands that Rome had recently conquered. There were cavalrymen from Gaul (ancient France), Holland, and Bulgaria, and expert archers from Syria. These troops were often sent to guard the vast frontier of the Empire.

Roman legions were commanded by legates, or generals, who represented the emperor. Each legate had a staff of six military tribunes, who in turn had authority over fifty-nine centurions, who commanded the centuries.

### *Military Service*

Every man who was a Roman citizen was required to serve in the military. The number of volunteer enlistments was high enough in itself, though, to defend the Empire. These volunteers were often farmers who worked in their fields in the spring and fall and served in the army during the summer.

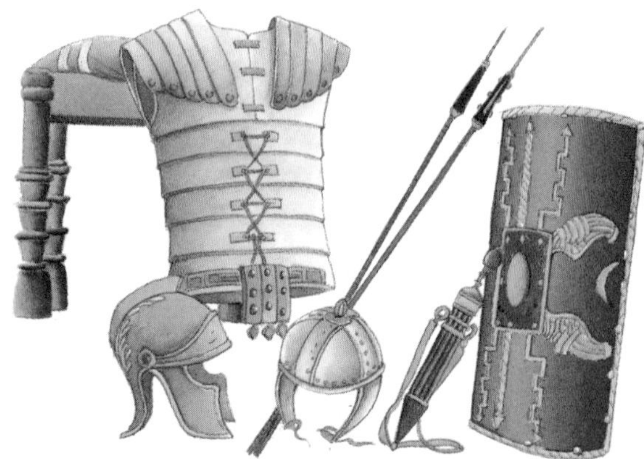

They were attracted by the regular salary and pension offered by army life. Military service lasted twenty years in the legions and twenty-five in the auxiliary regiments.

When soldiers were not actively engaged in battle, they performed drills, went on long marches, and built roads and fortifications along the thousands of miles of the Empire's frontier. They also labored on public projects, such as aqueducts, which

were built to carry water, and amphitheaters, enormous outdoor stadiums where the public gathered to watch spectacles.

*Storming the Towns*

Soldiers headed into battle with a long javelin, a dagger with a double-edged blade called a Spanish sword, and a short sword, or *gladius*. They wore a helmet, a breastplate made from strips of metal or leather, and leg protectors called *greaves*. A rectangular wooden shield with a metal cover over the handle protected soldiers from the enemy and served as a weapon in hand-to-hand combat. *Velites,* or light-armed infantrymen, were equipped with small, round shields, leather helmets, and javelins.

When Roman soldiers prepared to attack, they formed what was called a *testudo,* or tortoise. Like tortoises shrinking back into their shells, they grouped together and held their shields flat up over

their heads to form a protective cover against spears hurled by the enemy. To break through city walls, they used a ram, or a long tree trunk suspended from a rope.

**Roman Camps**

*Roman military camps were roughly 600 yards (550 meters) wide and 875 feet (800 meters) long. Camps were organized along two wide, perpendicular roads. An altar was built where the roads intersected, and the tents of the general and his staff were set up nearby. A cage containing holy geese was located at this important crossroads. Roman generals would allow their troops to engage in battle only if the holy geese ate with a healthy appetite.*

Roman soldiers also had sophisticated artillery. Catapults were devices much like giant slingshots that hurled stones and arrows at enemy cities. An onager was a heavy catapult that could shoot huge stones up to 980 feet (300 meters).

## THE ROMAN PEACE

During their many military campaigns in foreign lands, the Romans sometimes came upon people such as the Palestinians, Mesopotamians, Egyptians, and Greeks whose civilizations were much older and more highly developed than theirs. In other parts of the world, such as in Gaul, Germany, and Spain, they faced cultures that were newer and less structured. They called these people "barbarians." To them they brought Roman law and the Roman way of life.

Written laws, or rights, were essential to the Romans. Roman law was at the heart of both the city's organization and the life of its citizens. The oldest laws dated back to 450 B.C. in the early days of the Republic. All that time, the accepted practices of society were collected in the Law of the Twelve Tables. Children were expected to learn this complicated legal text by heart.

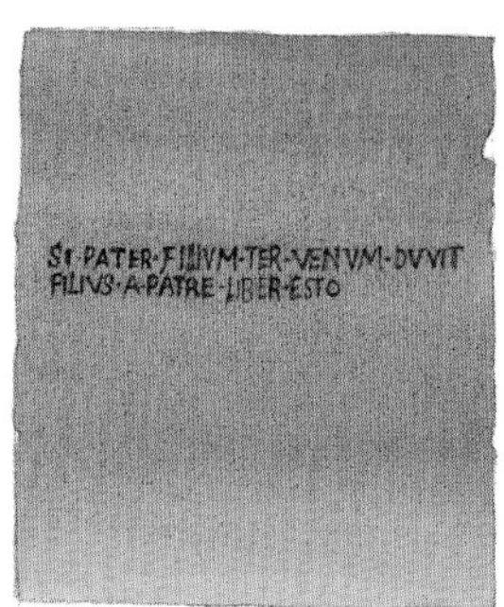


In the Republic, the law was open to the interpretations of lawyers and judges. As more and more land fell under Roman rule, the law took into account the different customs of the many peoples who lived in the Roman provinces.

During the Empire, though, as the size of the Roman world increased even more, the word of the emperor became the source of all law. This centralized authority allowed the Romans to secure peace and stability throughout an enormous area for over four hundred years.

### *Prosperous Times*

The two centuries in the beginning of the Christian era marked the Golden Age of the Roman Empire. For the first time in history, all of the lands surrounding the Mediterranean Sea were at peace. During this Golden Age—also known as the Pax Romana, or the Roman Peace—agriculture, industry, and commerce flourished.

**Connected by Road**

*Paved roadways cut across the Empire from north to south and from east to west. Agrippa (63–12 B.C.) organized a network of roads in Gaul. Trajan later developed similar roads through Spain and the Balkans. Finally, Hadrian developed the roads in Great Britain and improved those already existing in Spain and Africa. These many roadways encouraged trade and allowed military troops to travel more easily.*

Merchandise was traded from one end of the Mediterranean to the other. Mines were exploited in the Roman provinces of Spain, Dacia (present-day Rumania), and Great Britain. In its port city of Alexandria, Egypt received and stored cotton, spices, pearls, and precious gems from India; myrrh, incense, and alabaster from Arabia; and silk from distant, mysterious China. Gaul sent horses, fabrics, and food to Italy. Rome received wheat, ivory, and marble from North Africa; and beautifully woven carpets and textiles from Asia Minor (present-day Turkey).

*A Guarded Peace*

The Roman Peace relied on a strong system of defense. Limes was a defensive border built to repel enemy invasions at the outermost reaches of the Empire. Emperor Hadrian (A.D. 117–138) was responsible for organizing and developing this system of protection. In Germania (today, northeastern France), legionnaires raised small stone forts and dug ditches to sink the foundations of sturdy stockades. In Asia Minor a defensive line was built through the mountainous regions of Lebanon and in the Anti-Lebanon mountains along the border between Syria and Lebanon. In North Africa, Romans founded colonies and established guard posts. In Great Britain, Roman soldiers erected Hadrian's Wall to keep out the Caledonians who lived in the unconquered land of Scotland.

**Hadrian's Wall**

*Hadrian's Wall, which still stands today, runs for roughly 75 miles (120 kilometers) along the Scottish border. It is 20 feet (6 meters) tall and 8 feet (2.5 meters) wide. Every mile, a fort built into the wall gave shelter to some one hundred soldiers.*

## ROMANS AT SEA

The Romans managed to build an entire empire around the Mediterranean, which they called *mare nostrum,* or "our sea." And yet, they were not a seafaring people. They were determined to learn, though, and so they did. They studied the discoveries about boatbuilding and navigation made by the Etruscans, Greeks, and Carthaginians. Their efforts paid off; in time, they conquered the sea.

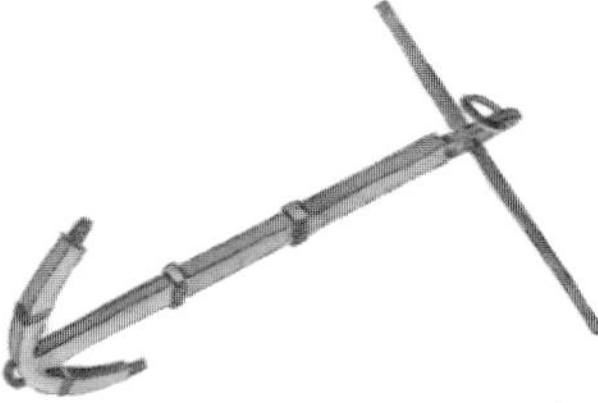

### *Cargo Ships*

Roman ships transporting goods back and forth across the Mediterranean were powered by several huge sails. Sailors on these cargo vessels used oars only to maneuver the ship into port or on days where there was no wind. The vessels were 80 to 100 feet (25 to 30 meters) long and 25 to 30 feet (8 to 10 meters) wide. They could hold from 110 to 180 tons of cargo. Hulls made of pine, fir, or oak were covered with planking and a tough, waterproof layer of lead sheeting.

The bow sat low in the water and was decorated with paintings of such things as eyes or Roman gods. The stern, on the other hand, was elevated. Two tillers shaped like shovels or spades served as a rudder. The steersman sat inside a small cabin or tent. In the center of the deck stood a tall mast supporting the large rectangular or trapezoid-shaped sail. Toward the bow, a smaller second sail was attached diagonally to the foremast.

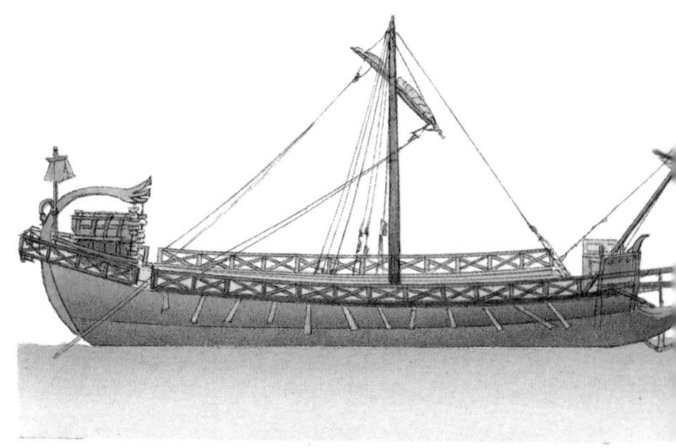

### *War Vessels*

Unlike merchant vessels, battleships were long and narrow. While some very light ships with only one row of oarsmen were to be found navigating the Mediterranean, every battleship had anywhere from two to six levels of oarsmen.

Quinqueremes, for example, had five levels of oars and were roughly 130 feet (40 meters) long and 20 to 23 feet (6 to 7 meters) wide. They could carry a crew of 300 sailors and 120 soldiers.

Warships were pointed at the bow end so that they could ram enemy vessels. A movable bridge, or platform, in midship was equipped with a grapnel, or *corvus,* that allowed two or more ships to be hitched together side by side. When ships were connected like this, naval combat looked much like warfare on the ground.

*Ports*

By trading with its provinces across the seas, the ever-expanding city of Rome received both necessary goods and luxury items. Mediterranean ports were constantly improved and enlarged. In planning new and impressive ports, Romans were inspired by the extraordinary port city of Alexandria, which had been built by the Greeks. The Romans built large ports, sometimes right on the seacoast, without the protection of a natural harbor. Strong breakwaters provided an area of calm seas where ships could dock. Docks were equipped with cables, arsenals, lighthouses, and warehouses. In Pozzuoli, a port on the southern coast of Italy, the Romans built an arched dike so that currents of water could pass underneath the dock without causing a build-up of sand.

**Roman Lighthouse**

*Lighthouses were tall square or circular towers that narrowed toward the top. Small fires on top of these structures burned constantly. Their light guided sea captains traveling at night, and during the day navigators relied on their smoke. One of the most famous Roman lighthouses was built by Caligula at Gesoriacum, now called Boulogne-sur-Mer, in France. This well-known 12-story lighthouse rose to a height of some 196 feet (60 meters).*

In the early days of the empire, Ostia, the natural harbor at the mouth of the Tiber river, was no longer large enough to handle the growing commercial traffic into Rome. Emperor Claudius had a large artificial harbor built a few miles to the north called Portus. A later emperor, Trajan, enlarged this new harbor once again in the second century.

## CITIZENS OF THE EMPIRE

Every Roman was proud to proclaim, "I am a Roman citizen." Citizenship implied the strong bond that tied individuals to their native town or region. Citizens of the city of Rome also remained loyal to the particular district in which they lived. In the beginning, Rome was not a single city; it was a cluster of individual settlements. And the most basic bond of all was the family. In fact, cities often grew out of associations of large families. Many of these families grew very powerful and played critical roles in the Republic's history.

Roman citizens had certain basic rights, which included the rights to vote, marry, and conduct business. By the time of the Empire, however, Roman citizens also had serious obligations, one of which was to defend the Empire by taking up arms.

### *Classes of Citizens*

Ancient Rome was a society broken up into many different classes. In the Republic, the ranking of citizens was fairly simple. Very few people belonged to the influential, monied upper class. The lower classes were divided into citizens and slaves.

**Women's Rights**

*Women living during the time of the Roman Empire were granted many new rights. One of the most important of these was the right to divorce, a liberty that had not been allowed in the Republic.*

In the time of the Empire, the class structure grew more complex. Augustus divided the upper-class citizens, called *honestiories,* into two orders. The wealthiest citizens made up the Senate, which still existed after the Republic, even though its actual influence had greatly lessened due to the all-powerful rule of Augustus. Consuls, magistrates, and provincial governors were selected from this group. But it was now the emperor who appointed the consuls and the senators, and in truth he relied more on his personal advisers than on these public servants.

### Slaves

*Slaves, who were bought and sold at special markets, had no rights whatsoever. They did all the tough, nasty jobs and household chores. The lives of many slaves improved in the Empire, when many owners granted their slaves freedom. Slaves living in the Empire could also buy emancipation, or freedom, with the wages they had earned.*

Other wealthy citizens with lesser fortunes were members of the equestrian order. Equestrians, or horsemen, served in the army and filled administrative positions in the government. In addition to these very fortunate members of society, a new commercial class of *equites* began to form from the landowners and businessmen who prospered along with the Empire.

And then there were a great many poor Romans. In spite of their hardship, though, many of these people refused to accept small jobs or occupations that they regarded as dishonorable. Such citizens preferred to do nothing. As many as 200,000 unemployed Romans took advantage of the emperor's distribution of free wheat. Poor citizens sometimes did chores for wealthy citizens who paid them with supplies or food. Those who lacked full-time jobs were anxious to cultivate relationships with the rich and powerful.

Roman citizens who worked for a living belonged to the social class of the *humiliores*. Craftsmen and shop owners, who belonged to this class, gathered together to form trade associations, or guilds. Other citizens of modest means worked in civil cohorts as watchmen or as low-level civil servants. Inhabitants of provincial towns and cities hoped to become Roman citizens. Roman emperors granted this much sought after title to single subjects or to entire towns that had proved their loyalty to the Empire. In A.D. 212 the emperor Caracalla granted Roman citizenship to all free men throughout the Empire. These people could then own land and seek protection under Roman law. The rulers hoped that widespread citizenship would create loyal subjects who would in turn help to hold the sprawling Roman lands together.

# ROMAN CITIES

At the center of the Empire lay its capital city of Rome. Between the eighth century B.C. and the first century A.D., Rome grew from a collection of sheepherders' huts into one of the most magnificent cities that the world has ever seen.

Rome was born on the Palatine, one of the seven hills that lay to the east of the Tiber river. Gradually villages formed on the other hills until, in the early fifth century B.C., four distinct regions had formed: Suburana, Esquiline, Collina, and Palatine. Peasants from these districts met together in a central meeting place, or forum, to exchange goods and ideas. In time, this open space was surrounded by markets, government buildings, and temples. The forum was the heart of Rome.

The Etruscans, who were great architects and engineers, dominated Rome in its early days. It was they who carefully planned and laid out Rome's city streets and built its sewers. Later, during the Republic, Rome's growth was completely unorganized. Julius Caesar, who ruled from 59 B.C. to 44 B.C., devised a detailed plan for the city's development. This plan was rediscovered and carried out by Augustus and his son-in-law Agrippa. They had the city, whose population had exploded, divided into fourteen districts.

Then, in A.D. 64, Rome was destroyed by a large fire and rebuilt again from scratch. In the second century, more than 1,200,000 people lived in the Empire's capital. No city on earth had ever been this large.

By the end of the Republic, the Roman forum had become too small for the many people who gathered there. In 54 B.C., Julius Caesar had a new forum built at the foot of the Capitoline hill. In the very center of the new forum stood the Temple of Venus Genitrix. Augustus later had two other forums built. But the largest imperial forum was built by Trajan. This forum had a monumental entrance arch, a large square surrounded by porticos, or covered walkways ringed with columns, a basilica, where the court and public assembly met, and two libraries. The famous Column of Trajan, built to honor the emperor, stood in front of the temple.

The Imperial Forums

*Busy Streets*

The big city's population was very heterogeneous, or mixed. Romans, Greeks, Orientals, Gauls, and Egyptians met and mingled in Rome's many pubs and inns.

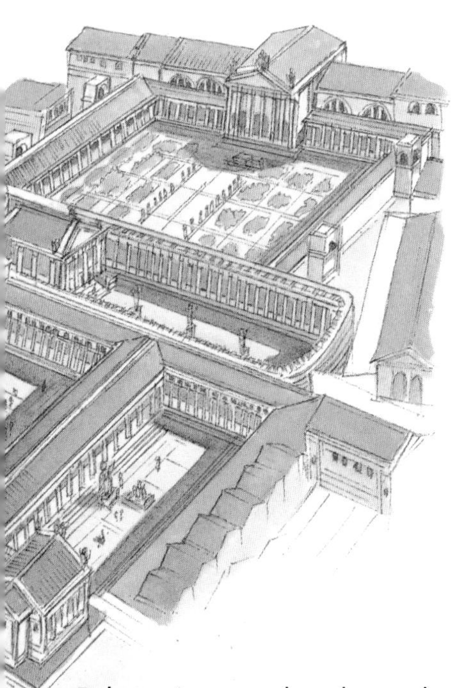

Palanquins—enclosed couches for one person carried by several men—and horse-drawn chariots crowded the roadways. Because the city streets were not lit at night, pedestrians and travelers carried lamps. Beneath the arcades, there were stalls of merchandise and strolling vendors peddling their wares. Stores were located on the main floors of large buildings. In the various boutiques, it was possible to find food, clothing, fabric, dishes, and even art objects. Rome had many tanneries, laundries, cleaners, bakeries, as well as workshops and studios for bronzesmiths, potters, blacksmiths, and cabinetmakers. There were also bankers' counters where travelers could exchange foreign currency.

*Security*

Augustus decreed that the city's security was to be maintained by four civil cohorts of Roman citizens commanded by the city prefect, or police chief, together with four to six tribunes. The Praetorian Guards were an elite cohort of soldiers who served as the emperor's bodyguards.

Augustus created seven cohorts of watchmen to serve as fire fighters. Special fire-fighting teams were in charge of operating the tricky water pumps and making sure that enough water was available at all times. Some of the fire fighters put out small fires with blankets drenched in vinegar while others held mattresses so that residents forced to jump from the windows of burning buildings could land safely.

*Food and Water Supplies*

A high-ranking civil servant in charge of the city's provisions saw that the city was stocked with enough wheat. Part of the city's grain was distributed free, or at very low prices, to poverty-stricken residents. From time to time, the poor were also given rations of oil and pork.

The problem of getting enough water to the city was solved by the building of aqueducts. At the end of the first century, nine of these enormous structures had already been erected. Trajan had an additional aqueduct built in the year 109, and Alexander Severus commissioned one at the beginning of the third century. Some aqueducts were designed to serve public buildings and baths. Others poured into water tanks, reservoirs, and the many public fountains where city residents came for their water. Rome and its one million inhabitants consumed an average of 260 million gallons (992,200 cubic meters) of water in the space of 24 hours.

**The Wall Around the City**

*During the first few centuries of Rome's history, while Romans were busy fighting the other peoples of the surrounding region of Latium, the city was protected by a wall said to have been built by Servius Tullius. In the third century A.D., the threat of barbarian invasions led the emperor Aurelian to build strong ramparts, or city walls, stretching for 11.7 miles (19 kilometers) around the city. The wall was 19.6 feet (6 meters) tall and 11.5 feet (3.5 meters) wide. Every 100 feet (29.6 meters) the wall was reinforced by a square lookout tower.*

## PUBLIC BUILDINGS

Roman cities were easy to recognize because they were full of splendid monuments. The cities of Italy, Gaul, Spain, and Africa were all built in the image of Rome.

Each of them housed a forum, a basilica, a Capitol, temples, public baths, theaters, and amphitheaters. These public buildings were small imitations of those found in the capital city.

*Roman Forums*

Each Roman city had a town square, or forum, where residents came together to see one another and conduct business. Forums were usually surrounded by porticos, and the shops were lined up against the inside walls so that passersby had more room to stroll and browse.

At one end of the forum stood a temple. This monument was dedicated to three gods: Jupiter, Juno, and Minerva. Worship of the emperor, however, eventually replaced the cult of Jupiter. In the second century A.D., the residents of Nimes, a city in the south of Gaul, dedicated their city's temple, the well-known Maison Carrée, to the grandsons and heirs of Augustus, Gaius, and Lucius Caesar. An altar for ritual sacrifices was built in front of the temple.

The basilica, which housed the city's commercial and public activities, ran along one side of the forum. The basilica also housed the rostrum, or platform, where the city magistrates sat to deliver justice.

Another large and important building dominated the forum: the *curia*. This was the workplace of the municipal magistrates, or *decurionis,* who were responsible for running the city. They represented different city districts just as Roman senators represented various regions of the Empire.

*Theaters and Amphitheaters*

Theaters and amphitheaters are among the best-preserved Roman monuments still standing today. In the Empire, each city had its own theater, which was usually open to the sky. The audience sat on a half circle of tiered seats around the stage. Actors entered the stage through doors in a massive stone wall that was decorated with statues and columns. Women were not allowed to sit near the stage because they might be tempted to run off with one of the actors!

Romans loved theatrical performances, but it was their passion for the competitions of the amphitheater that characterized Roman civilization. Architects created innovative structures that allowed crowds of hundreds of thousands of people to enter and exit through many arched vaults. These vaults also provided a very strong support for the terrific weight of the tiered stone seats that rested on top of them.

*Roman Baths*

Every large city in the Empire had its public bathhouse. These establishments were an integral part of Roman life. People used them to wash themselves, since private homes almost never had their own baths. They also went to the baths to relax, chat with their friends, exercise, play games, listen to music, and even to read and look at art. While the forum remained the commercial center of the city, it was in the baths that the complex web of social interactions was spun.

Visitors left their clothes on shelves in the changing rooms before entering a sweating-room called the *sudarium*. After working up a heavy sweat, they went into the *caldarium* to rinse off in a warm bath. From there they moved into a warm room called the *tepidarium* before splashing into cold baths, or *frigidarium*.

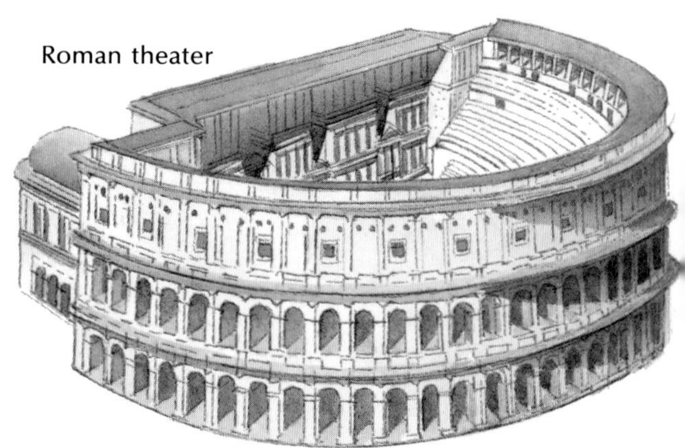

**Roman theater**

People sweated in the hot steam to cleanse the pores of their skin. They rubbed themselves with olive oil instead of soap, which was an oddity in ancient Rome. The baths were also a way to relax tense muscles. People often requested a massage after their steam bath. Skilled masseurs rubbed them down with special oils and perfumes.

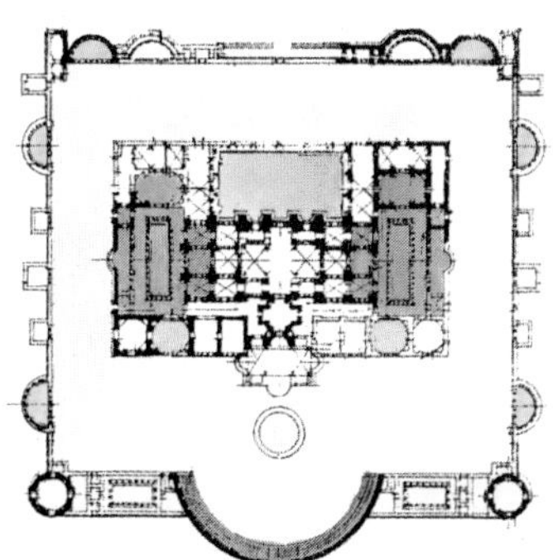

Floor plan of a bathhouse

Gardens

- Baths and outdoor pool
- Indoor and outdoor palaestrae
- Rooms for social gatherings and exhibits
- Greek and Latin library
- Areas for outdoor concerts and plays

These enormous complexes were heated by wood-burning furnaces located in the basement. Hot air was funneled through the spaces formed between layers of tiles behind the walls of the bathhouse and beneath its floors. This heat might be either dry or steamy. It was also used to warm large outdoor swimming pools.

Bathing was not the only activity available at the baths. Gymnasiums and wrestling palaestrae, or schools, were for physically active people, while the baths' libraries and salons were for the spiritually minded. People came to the bathhouses to listen to concert music and to hear poets recite their new works. Social gatherings were held in sumptuous rooms decorated with mosaics and statues.

## MASTERFUL BUILDERS

C. Julius Lacer, an architect from the Roman province of Lusitania in Spain, inscribed the following words into the arched stone bridge he had just completed in Alcántara: "[This achievement will] last forever through the ages." He was right to be proud. His bridge spans the Tagus river today.

The two-thousand-year-old skeletal remains of baths, columns, archways, porticos, walls, theaters, amphitheaters, and bridges in Italy, Greece, Egypt, and Asia Minor are evidence of the skill and vision of Roman builders. The great chariot race track of Circus Maximus in Rome seated 250,000 spectators, more than any stadium holds today. The Coliseum, an oval amphitheater completed in A.D. 80, and the Pantheon, a temple dedicated to the gods, are giant specters in the city of Rome today.

Buildings were made of stone, marble, fired bricks, and even concrete. From the Etruscans, the Romans learned the technique of cutting stone into parallelepipeds, six-faced square or rectangular blocks, which they fitted together side by side into horizontal rows.

It was undoubtedly the Etruscans who also passed on their knowledge of vaults, arched or dome-shaped structures that became the trademark of Roman builders. Vaults allowed for the construction of stronger bridges than had ever been built before. Domes—vaults resting on a circular base—formed the roofs or ceilings of many Roman buildings.

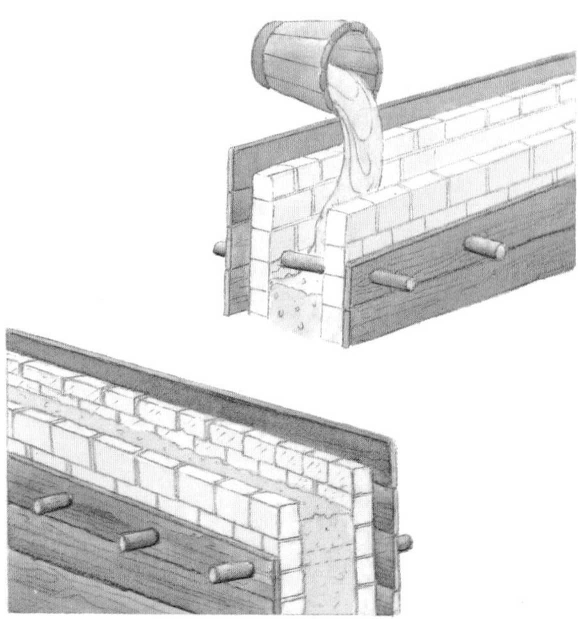

*Cement, a Roman Invention*

It was Roman architects who first used cement to bind bricks and stones together. They mixed mortar (three measures of sand to one measure of lime) with a blend of stone and brick fragments. Cement was both economical and practical. It created a strong foundation that allowed builders to expand their construction in terms of both size and design.

Roman builders hid the ugly cement beneath a variety of coatings. Early builders simply assembled small, irregularly shaped stone blocks to create a flat surface. Later, masons cut small stone cubes of similar sizes and shapes out of tuff, a rock formed from volcanic material. They placed them on the diagonal so that the wall's face looked like a net.

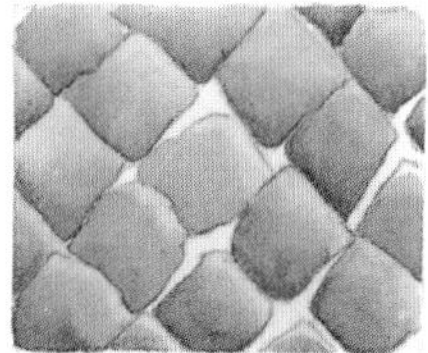

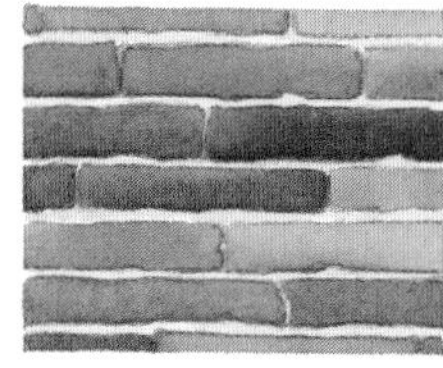

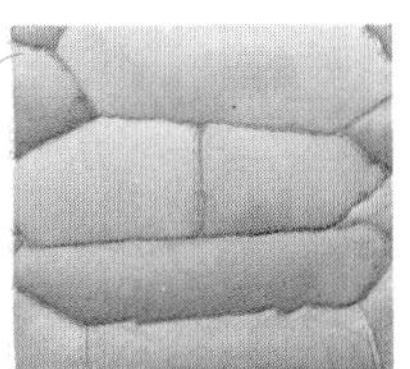

**The Pantheon**

*The Pantheon's dome, which is 142 feet (43.2 meters) high, is the second tallest ever built. The dome at Saint Peter's Basilica in Rome is the world's tallest. The height of the Pantheon's dome impressed the painter and sculptor Michelangelo. Visitors still find it amazing today.*

During the reign of Tiberius (A.D. 14–37), these small blocks were replaced by layers of brick. The imperial palaces on the Palatine Hill, the great public baths, and all the Roman temples were built using this technique. From the fourth century on, horizontal layers of brick were alternated with stone cubes.

*Scaffolding*

An ancient bas-relief, a sculpture carved in a flat surface, has shown researchers how elevating machines allowed Roman builders to lift heavy stone blocks high into the air. The elevator, suspended by ropes, was set in motion by a large wheel. Men marching inside this early version of the treadmill made it go around. This useful invention was rediscovered by Renaissance architects about fifteen hundred years later.

## PRIVATE HOMES

In the early days of the Republic the house, or *domus,* was built around a square courtyard called an *atrium* containing a pool of water. This central basin, or *impluvium,* collected the rainwater that fell from the house's inward slanting roof.

Off the central courtyard were the kitchen, dining room, and bedrooms. Toward the back of the house was the *tablinum,* a private room for the father of the family, and a small garden.

Beginning in the second century B.C., the *peristyle* house replaced the atrium. A peristyle was a colonnaded inner courtyard built behind the tablinum. In these new houses, a series of beautifully decorated rooms—including bedrooms, bathrooms, a dining room, and library—were built around an interior garden decorated with fountains and statues. The rooms received light from the peristyle. None of the house's windows opened onto the street.

In the homes of wealthy Romans there were beds in every room! Of course, some of these were for sleeping, but those in the other rooms of the house were used for writing and reading. Men even reclined on them in the dining room. Actually, for the Romans these beds served as couches. Chairs were not part of everyday life. They were reserved strictly for women, honored guests, and the elderly. When people weren't relaxing on beds, they sat on small folding stools.

Floor plan of a house

Beds were made of wood decorated with bronze. Some were even carved from stone and trimmed with cushions to soften them. People spent fortunes on elegant tables with bronze tops or surfaces inlaid with mar-

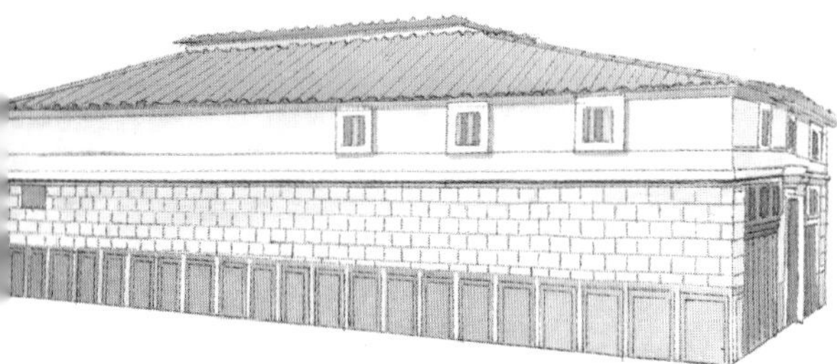

quetry, elaborate patterns created with wood, ivory, or shells.

Rooms did not usually hold much furniture. Floors, though, might be inlaid with colorful mosaics or covered with patterned carpets. Walls were often decorated with painted murals and wall hangings.

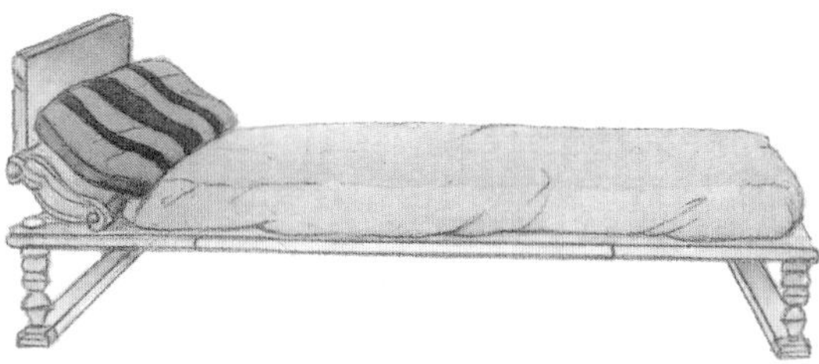

*Apartment Living*

Single-family homes were a luxury. In Rome, in its port city of Ostia, as well as in the biggest provincial cities, Romans lived literally on top of one another in large five- or six-story buildings. These "apartment houses," which were 59 to 65 feet (18 to 20 meters) tall, were called *insulae*.

**Light**

*Romans lit the rooms of their houses and apartments with modest oil lamps or wax candles placed in candlesticks. Oil lamps were also used as streetlights.*

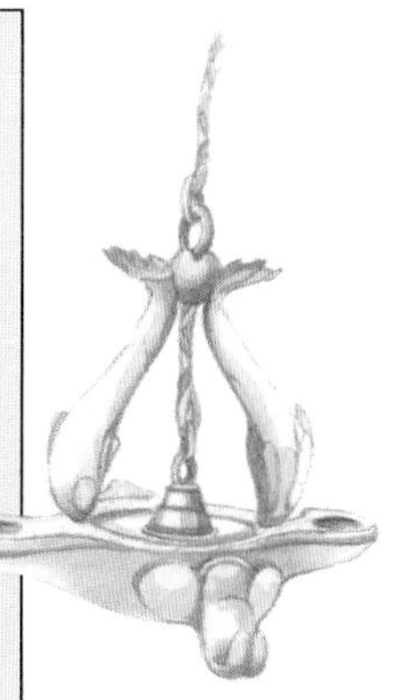

In the fourth century, the city of Rome had 45,000 insulae and only 1,800 domus. On the main floor of such buildings there were shops and boutiques. The most elegant apartments opened onto interior courtyards, which were sometimes very pretty. There were apartments on the upper floors, which often had wood or masonry balconies overlooking the street. The building's ground floor was often lined with covered archways. Roofs were generally made of tile. Two or three apartment houses sometimes formed a group so that common services such as fountains, baths, toilets, and laundries could be shared by a large number of people. Otherwise, apartment dwellers had to use public fountains and latrines. And then they could also go to the public baths.

# THE PROVINCES

The first Romans herded sheep and cultivated enough soil to grow crops for their own survival. They were deeply tied to the land. In fact, the earliest original writing that we have found in Latin is a manual on agriculture by Cato the Elder, a statesman who lived from 234 B.C. to 149 B.C.

Early farmers lived in small huts or ramshackle cottages made by stacking up materials to form walls around an inner courtyard.

As the Empire expanded to include more and more territory, many farmers joined the Roman legions and spent their lives fighting abroad. Often they had to sell their land. A single wealthy Roman would buy up many small plots and raise crops and animals to sell for a profit. Gradually the rustic countryside became dotted with estates, or *villas*.

Rustic villas began to appear toward the end of the first century B.C. The ruins of one of the most beautiful of these can be seen today at Boscoreale, near Pompeii. The villa's rooms filled only one quarter of the entire space. The spacious and impressive villa was built with two large interior courtyards. One of these contained a water tank and a watering trough. The other held rows of earthenware jars buried underground where perishable foods and supplies could be safely stored.

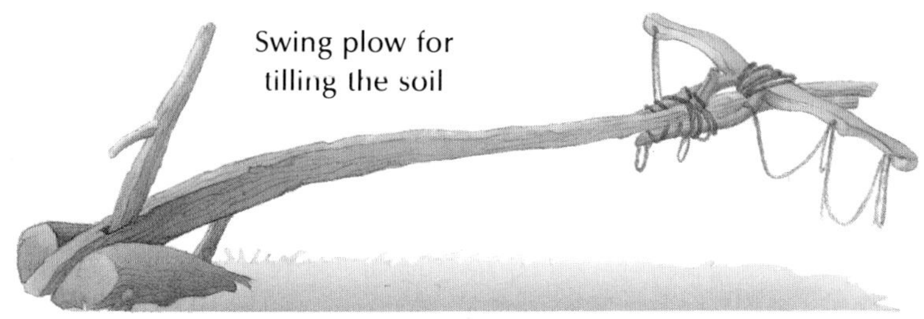
Swing plow for tilling the soil

**Pliny the Younger's Letter**

*"Here I am in my villa in Tuscany. I hunt and I study, sometimes at the same time, sometimes one right after the other. I am still unable to decide, however, which is more difficult to hunt: game or ideas?"*

On one side of the villa, there were stables and sleeping rooms for the slaves, as well as the kitchen, bathrooms, toilets, toolshed, oven, and a bakery complete with a millstone. On the other side of the residence were wine presses and large containers in which wine was stored, water tanks, grain mills, and oil presses. A staircase in the kitchen led up to the first floor and the master's bedroom.

## FARMING THE LAND

Roman farmers grew grain such as wheat and barley, grapes to make wine, and a wide variety of vegetables, including beans, lentils, cabbage, and leeks. They grew and harvested wild olives, and their orchards contained many different kinds of fruit trees. Ancient farmers knew to rotate their crops from year to year. They also knew to let cultivated land lie fallow for a while so that nutrients would return to the soil. Dung, ashes, and manure were used to fertilize the fields.

Cattle were used to draw heavy loads, and from cows' milk came cheese. Farmers raised mules, pigs, and horses in addition to sheep for wool, and goats for milk. They also raised bees for honey, which they used as a sweetener instead of sugar.

Farmyards began to develop in the early days of the Empire. Geese, chicken, pheasants, peacocks, and cranes were popular barnyard animals.

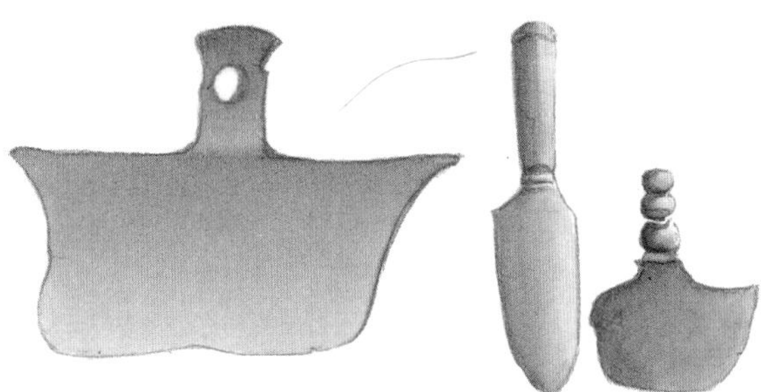
*Tools*

In ancient Rome, there was no shortage of tools. Romans worked with double-edged pickaxes, scythes, hoes, hatchets, billhooks (pruning tools with hooked blades), small saws to trim vines, and dibbles, or trowels, to make holes in the ground for planting. The swing plow was used for shallow digging in the fields. Farmers used flails, or wooden sticks, to thresh wheat. Sometimes, though, it was easier for large farm animals to simply crush the ears of wheat by stamping on them.

## TRAVELING THROUGH THE LAND

When Romans traveled long distances they wore short tunics and hooded coats that protected them from the wind and cold. Their baggage consisted of an animal skin or wool pouch and a string bag or wooden crate. Travelers were recognizable by the purses they attached to their belts to hold money and precious objects.

When Romans set out on long journeys, they carried a walking stick to scare away stray dogs and thieves. Traveling along deserted roadways could be risky. Well-equipped travelers carried informative guide books and maps, some of which were more detailed than others.

Most Romans traveled by foot, but some of them rented horses. Those who needed to get somewhere quickly rode in two-wheeled carriages modeled after Gallic War chariots. *Cisiūm,* or two-wheeled vehicles made of wicker, were lighter and even faster. Four-wheeled vehicles transported passengers with baggage. In luxury vehicles called *carrucae,* passengers could lie down and go to sleep.

For short journeys within the city, people rode in sedan chairs or litters, couches equipped with comfortable cushions.

People often had to journey by sea. Because there were no passenger ships, however, travelers had to secure an empty spot on a trading vessel. Very wealthy passengers could afford to ride in their own personal boats, called galleys. These were commonly propelled by oars, and slaves did the rowing.

### *Sleeping Away from Home*

Wealthy Romans traveling long distances often relied on the hospitality of friends and acquaintances, who would invite them into their homes to spend the night. When travelers didn't know anyone in the area they sometimes slept in their vehicles. Magistrates and other government officials stayed

in hostelries maintained especially for their use. Only travelers with very little money chose to spend the night in roadside inns, or *cauponae*. These inns were miserable, uncomfortable places to stay, and travelers were likely to be robbed in their sleep. Inn keepers were often said to be dishonest men and thieves.

*Tourists in the Ancient World*

Many Romans traveled for business reasons. But others chose to vacation by exploring unknown lands, just as we do today. The Roman tourist industry flourished under the Empire. People flocked to look at the pyramids in Egypt, strolled through foreign towns on the coast of Asia Minor, and visited the Greek Islands in the Aegean Sea.

Some travelers even journeyed beyond the bounds of the Empire. Often, they were driven by curiosity. In A.D. 37, for example, the father-in-law of Tacitus the historian set off to explore the coast of Scotland. In that same year, an exploratory mission was sent as far as China.

**Mail**

*In the Empire, couriers carrying messages in leather saddlebags covered great distances on horseback. Every 8 miles (13 kilometers) they came upon special posts, or stopping places, where they could exchange their tired, thirsty horses for fresh ones. From the second century on, every citizen in the Roman Empire could take advantage of this postal system. Letters were written on rolled and sealed papyrus sheets.*

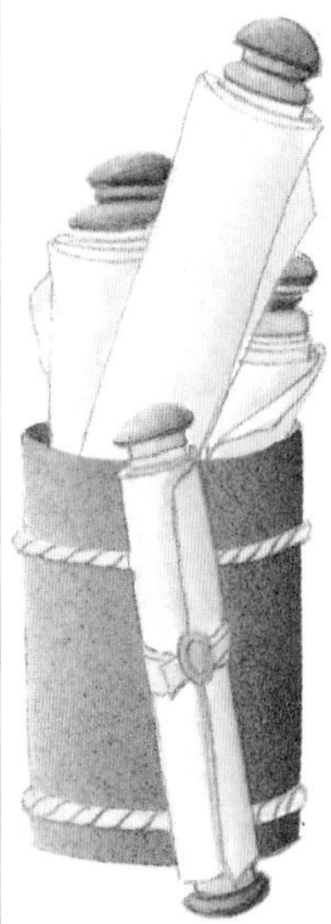

# A ROMAN CHILDHOOD

The family was very important to Romans. And yet, human life was not valued in the same way as it is today. In the early days of the Republic, parents had the right to do away with children who were sickly at birth, malformed, or simply too difficult to take care of. Gradually, these ancient traditions, common to many early communities, were replaced by more humane attitudes. This was partly due to the spread of Christianity, which viewed human life as sacred.

The father of the household, or *paterfamilias,* held the power of life and death over everyone in the household, including his wife. But in most families, this power was never put into practice. On the whole, children worked at their lessons and played games in much the same way that modern

children do. Children of slaves, though, were born into slavery and made to work terribly hard for long hours. These were the unlucky ones.

## YOUNG ROMANS AT SCHOOL

Roman schools were called *ludī,* a term that meant play and amusement as well as the place where children learned. In fact, Romans thought of the time they devoted to study as a form of leisure.

Certain educational methods took the form of games. For example, small sweet candies called *crustulae,* shaped like the letters of the alphabet, were designed to help children learn to read and write.

Roman parents were responsible for providing their children with an education. Fathers taught their sons how to read and write and how to prepare for military service. Young boys learned from their fathers how to swim, run, and handle weapons. Mothers showed their daughters how to spin wool and keep house.

Wealthy Romans entrusted their children's education to special slaves called pedagogues who were often of Greek origin. In 250 B.C., one such pedagogue, Livius Andronicus, translated Homer's epic poem *The Odyssey* into Latin to better explain it to his students. This was the first work of literature translated from Greek into Latin.

**Strict Discipline**

*Naughty students were punished physically. Children tried to behave because they were afraid of being hit with a rod or beaten with a whip. The master's rod, or* ferula, *was an important symbol of his authority.*

Toward the end of the Republic, the pedagogue's role was to accompany children to and from school and to make them recite their lessons out loud.

*How Long Did Studies Last?*

In the Empire, there were three levels of education. From the ages of seven to twelve students took lessons from the *magister,* or schoolmaster, who taught reading, writing, and mathematics.

From the ages of twelve to seventeen, students went to grammar school, *grammaticus,* where they studied the great poets of Greek and Latin literature (Homer, Horace, and Virgil). They learned the poems by heart and wrote compositions about what they meant. Memorization was an important part of their education.

At the age of seventeen, adolescents studied with a rhetorician, a master of writing and public speaking. He taught them the art of writing speeches on various topics. This was an important skill because Romans, whether they were magistrates, lawyers, or members of the military, were often called upon to address their fellow men in public. The wealthiest students later went off to Greece to study with a philosopher.

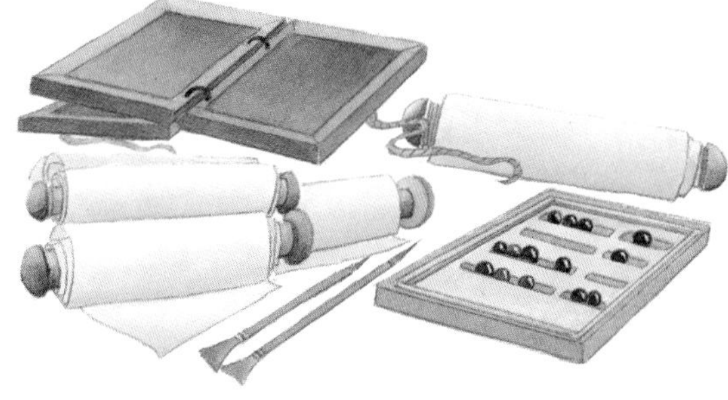

*In the Classroom*

Classes were often held outdoors or in the shade of the porticos. Sometimes, however, teachers gave lessons in shops where they could set up benches or stools for the children and chairs for themselves. Children carried *capsae,* or cases full of school supplies. They wrote on wooden tablets coated with a layer of soft wax. Letters and words were traced into the wax with the sharp tip of a metal or ivory tube whose blunt end served as an eraser.

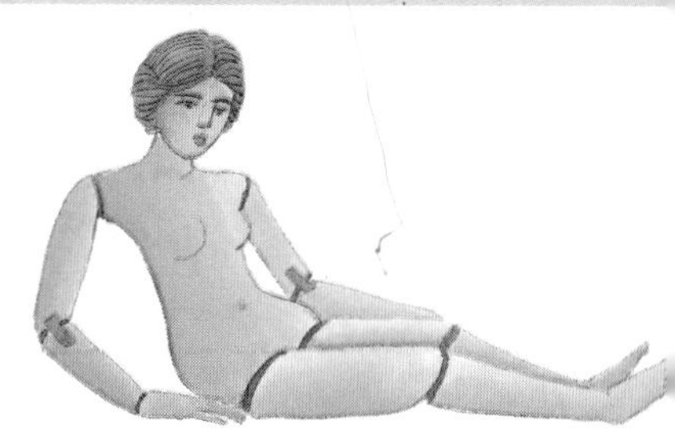

Students learning to count worked with abacuses. Masters provided a table where children could solve elementary math problems or work on their geometry with cubes and spheres. Geographical maps and mythological tables were hung around the walls of the classroom for children to study and discuss. The classroom also contained busts of poets and philosophers.

## CHILDREN AT PLAY

Romans liked to play games. When adults went to visit friends or family members, they often played chess or backgammon. Dice and knucklebones (jacks made out of dried animal bones) were also popular. Children had a wide variety of games and toys to choose from, too.

Around their necks, infants wore toy rattles, figurines with stone pellets, bells, or rings inside them that crackled or tinkled when they were touched. These noisemakers, called *crepundiae,* also served as amulets, or charms, against evil or injury.

Vases serving as piggybanks, masks made of ivory or terra-cotta, letters cut from ivory, lead figurines shaped like gods, and miniature sacrificial instruments were also thought to bring good luck.

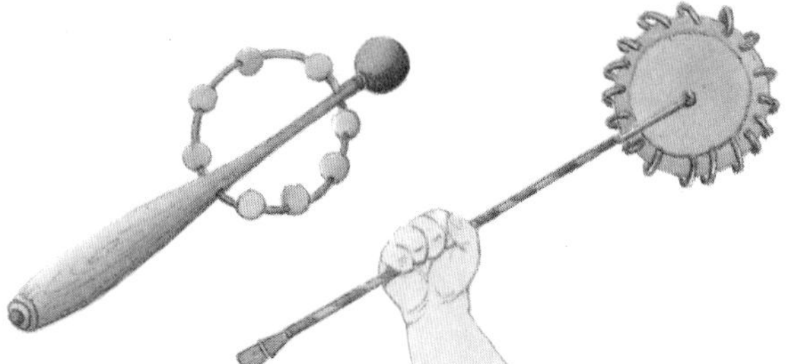

### *Popular Games*

Scholars today know a lot about the kinds of toys and games Romans liked to play because they were represented in paintings and bas-reliefs. Images of scooters, jump-ropes, kites, yo-yos, swings, and children playing leapfrog appear over and over again. Small stones, glass, and little pottery balls were used as marbles. Knucklebones was one of the most popular games. Small wooden tops were made to spin by pulling a leather strap.

The most popular toys appear to have been wooden or terra-cotta animals on wheels that children pulled along behind them. Lucky children rode in small cars or go-carts hitched to the family goat, pony, or dog.

**Hoops for Everyone!**

*Children, teenagers, and even some adults loved playing with hoops. Most hoops were made from light-weight wooden sticks that could be bent without breaking. Wicker twigs were tied around the wood to make it hold its circular form. Other hoops were made of metal, bronze, or iron.*

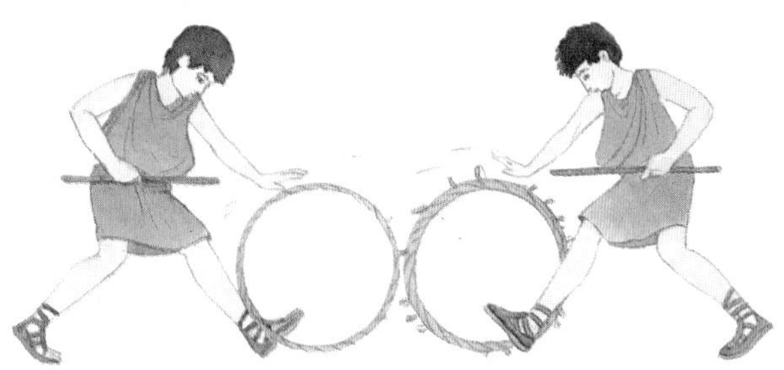

Only a few Roman rag dolls and figurines made of wax have been preserved. Sturdy dolls made of terra-cotta, wood, bone, or ivory, however, have stood the test of time. Some ancient Roman dolls even had movable arms and legs. The doll industry flourished in the third century A.D.

Children had pets to play with, too. Cats were a common sight in Roman households, as were exotic caged birds. Families kept many different breeds of dogs. Some of them were lap dogs, while others were trained to guard the home. In country villas, dogs were often used for the hunt. Identity tags have been found with the names of owners printed on them, in case the dogs got lost.

### *Boys and Girls Playing Together*

Ovid, in one of his well-known poems, gave a speaking role to a walnut tree. The unhappy old tree complained that he was the most ill-treated of all trees because children were constantly shaking him down and stealing his walnuts.

Walnuts were used in many different games of skill and chance. The emperor Augustus himself liked to join the children who grew up in the palace in their games with walnuts.

Roman boys and girls enjoyed playing ball. Balls were often round, fabric pouches stuffed with horsehair. Small, easy-to-catch balls were filled with sand, while others were stuffed with fur. Medium-sized balls were filled with feathers, and large playing balls were filled with nothing but air. There was no lack of variety.

**Odd or Even**

*The very popular game "odd or even" was easy to play. One child held stones, coins, almonds, or knucklebones in a closed fist. The other player had to guess whether the closed hand contained an even or odd number of objects.*

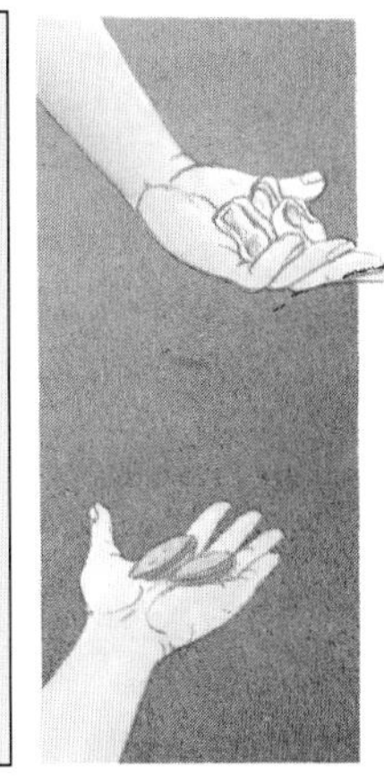

# ROMAN DRESS

In his manual on agriculture, Cato the Elder wrote, "Tunics, togas, blankets, smocks and shoes should be bought in Rome." It would appear that as early as the second century B.C. a retail clothing trade had been established in the Republic.

From some inscriptions, we have learned that there was also quite a trade in used clothes, which people bought for cheap prices and turned into blankets and wrappings. Much of the fabric, such as wool, linen, and fine silks and furs, would have been imported.

Cobblers made shoes in small workshops. Some made men's shoes and heavy boots out of leather, while others specialized in women's shoes or slippers, which were woven out of plant fibers.

Styles of dress varied over the centuries, but on the whole Romans dressed simply. Both men and women wore tunics, loose gowns of wool or linen. Pants were thought of as an unmanly fashion worn only by foreigners! And yet, in spite of the simplicity of Roman clothing, slight differences in the cut or color of a garment could say a lot about the social or political position of its wearer. Women also varied their appearance by using makeup and wearing jewelry.

For a toga, a large piece of cloth

Romans wore togas over their tunics on formal occasions. Togas were cut from large semicircular pieces of fabric. The many folds of cloth that wrapped around the body made them heavy and cumbersome to wear.

As for everyday wear, ordinary citizens, freedmen and freedwomen (slaves, who had either bought or been granted their freedom), and slaves alike wore matching tunics. These were made from two rectangles of wool sewn together at the shoulders with openings for the head and arms. Belts worn at the waist allowed men to hitch up the long fabric that would otherwise hang to their calves. The fullness of the fabric meant that men's arms were covered with soft, elegant pleats. Julius Caesar liked to wear tunics decorated with fringe and braid.

### *Women's Clothing*

Well-to-do women wore longer tunics than men. Over their tunics, they wore long pleated robes called *stolae* that were tight-fitting at the waist and decorated along the

> **In Praise of Mothers**
>
> *Women with three or more children wore distinctive, elegant clothing. It was Augustus who initiated this custom as a way of encouraging Romans to have lots of children.*

bottom with a band of red fabric or embroidery. Such fancy robes made it possible to distinguish wealthy Roman women from lower-class women and slaves. Unlike togas, these elegant robes had sleeves and were not draped.

*Coats*

To protect themselves from the rain and cold, Romans wore short, dark, woolen coverings called *lacernae.* These hooded coats, which were worn over togas, attached at the shoulder or buckled under the chin. Lacernae were cut from bright colored fabrics and decorated with embroidery or fringe.

Simpler overcoats called *paenulae* were worn for traveling. These jackets were made from a circular piece of fabric with a hole cut in the center for the head. They were often made with hoods. Paenulae made from animal skins were both warm and waterproof.

*Accessories*

Under their togas, Romans wore woolen undershirts as well as tunics. These undergarments, which sometimes had sleeves, were made from two simple pieces of fabric sewn together. Women wrapped their chests with cloth bands that served as brassieres.

Roman men wore boots or sandals when they went outdoors and changed into slippers when they returned home. Women's

boots were lighter versions of those worn by men and were often brightly colored and decorated with pearls or precious gems.

In the country, poor peasants and slaves wore wooden clogs or simply wrapped their feet with animal skins or coarse wool rags.

*Elegant Roman Women*

In the Empire, the condition of women changed considerably. During that period, women were no longer required to stay at home with servants, spinning wool and devoting themselves entirely to their children's education. Women even began attending shows given in amphitheaters.

As the styles and tastes of the eastern part of the Empire began to spread to the west, wealth and luxury items gained importance. Women began to spend more time getting dressed, applying makeup, and caring for their bodies.

Roman women were very fond of cosmetics. Wealthy women did not apply their own makeup in the morning; servants did this for them. Pale complexions were the fashion. To achieve this delicate look, servants spread white pasty creams made from powdered chalk or lead on the faces and arms of their mistresses. (No one knew at the time that some of these cosmetics, such as those made from lead, were poisonous.) They also applied eyeliner and darkened eyebrows with a compound made of ash. Cheeks and lips were colored with a red iron ore called ocher. The women kept their creams and powders in collections of ceramic pots and alabaster flasks and in special little round boxes.

### *Jewelry*

After their makeup had been put on, women selected an assortment of rings and earrings. They attached necklaces and small chains around their necks and bracelets around their wrists and ankles. Roman women enjoyed wearing large decorative pendants on their chests as well. Pins and buckles designed to attach clothing were often made of precious gems. Women also wore pretty diadems, or jeweled crowns, in their hair.

When elegant Roman women went out to meet their friends in the evening, they wrapped themselves in floor-length shawls and tied long scarves around their heads. Sometimes they wore large, brightly colored, and carefully pleated coats called *pallae*.

## Combs

*Combs made of bronze, ivory, shell, or animal horn were an important women's accessory. Combs usually had two distinct layers: one where the teeth were placed tightly together, and another where they were far apart.*

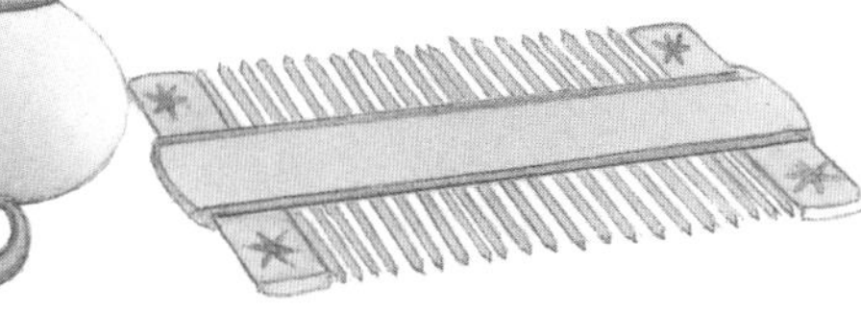

*Hairstyles*

In the Republic, women did not fuss with their hair. They parted it down the middle and pulled it back into a bun. But for Roman women who lived during the Empire, hairstyles were a critical element in their appearance.

At the beginning of the second century, hairstyles became more and more complicated, and often involved elaborate constructions built with curls. The renowned satiric poet Juvenal thought that the contrast between the size of small ladies and their enormous, bouffant hairstyles was ridiculous. He wrote, "There are so many layers, and so many parts to the construction of that edifice that heightens and enlarges her head! From the front you would think she was Andromache [a Greek heroine], but seen from the back, she looks so much smaller that you take her to be another woman."

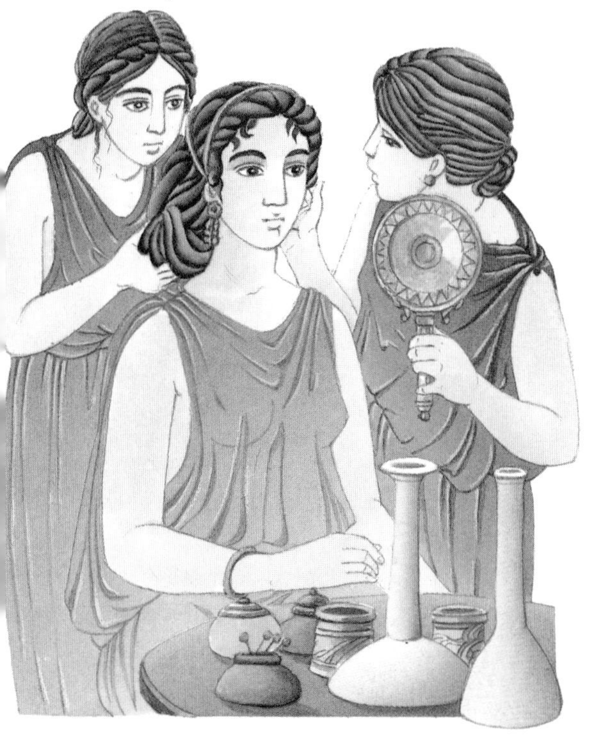

## Mirrors

*Mirrors were generally square and made from bronze or silver. By the fifth century A.D., they were made from blown glass attached to a flat metal surface.*

# FOOD AND DRINK

Wealthy Romans gained a reputation for indulging in lavish banquets where guests ate and drank themselves into a stupor. But these stories do not draw an accurate picture of the way most Romans lived. Middle- and lower-class people led a simple life.

At that time, potatoes and tomatoes were unknown outside of the Americas. The Romans had not yet discovered pasta. And many people could not afford to eat meat very often. Even if they could afford to eat meat or fish, they had trouble keeping it fresh, since there was no refrigeration. Ice cubes were an extravagance that involved elaborate systems of preservation and so were reserved for the wealthy few.

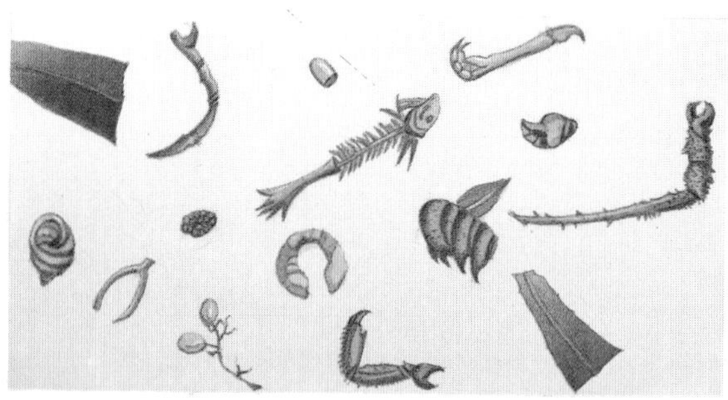

As the Empire spread east, Romans discovered new ways of cooking the foods that were available and new spices to add flavor to sauces and the wheat porridge that was the staple diet for many people.

## THREE MEALS A DAY

Romans didn't eat much for the first two meals of the day. Breakfast (*ientaculum*) consisted of bread dipped in wine, or spread with garlic, salt, or cheese. Schoolchildren left home in the morning with a wheat biscuit clutched in their hands. Lunch (*prandium*), which was served between 11:30 and noon, was usually a quick meal consisting of cold meat or fish, vegetables, eggs, mushrooms, fruits, and a bit of wine. The only large meal of the day was dinner (*cena*). This was served when the day's work was finished. Poor people lived on wheat. They generally ate a bowl of porridge made from boiled ground wheat for their dinner, flavoring its bland taste with many different things: herbs, olives, thyme, oregano, or perhaps a few vegetables, mushrooms, or a little meat.

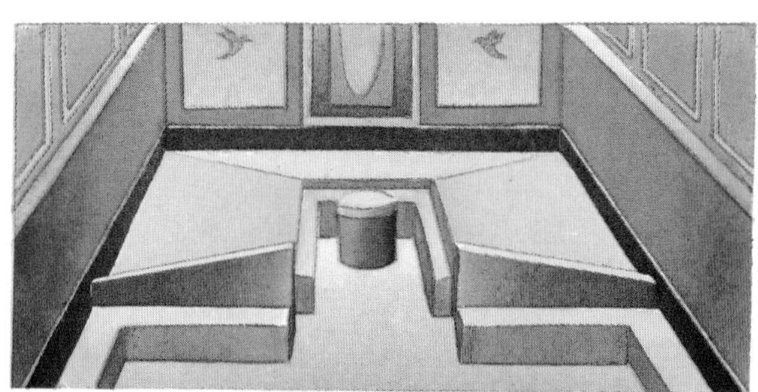

During the first centuries of the Empire, Romans had not yet begun to eat bread. When bread was introduced, though, it gradually replaced the traditional wheat porridge. Farmers and country people tended to make their own tough, black bread, while those who could afford it bought soft white bread from bakers in town.

## SPECIAL MEALS

On special occasions, such as dinner parties, or birthdays or weddings, meals were much more elaborate and varied. Lots of appetizers were served: salads, radishes, eggs, oysters, and sardines. This was often followed by a drink of wine diluted with water and sweetened with honey. There might be as many as six or seven main courses.

The main courses could include different kinds of poultry—chicken, goose, ostrich, duck, partridge, pheasant, dove, and, on very special evenings, peacock. Meat dishes might be boar, beef, venison, mutton, lamb, pig, hare, or even dormouse. And then there was often fish.

Both fresh and saltwater fish were served. Romans had recipes for the preparation of more than one hundred species. Popular fish from the Mediterranean were bass, mullet, mackerel, tuna, sole, prawn, and eel. At the beginning and end of meals it was common to have seafood and shellfish. Oysters were considered a delicacy, much as they are today. Lake and river fish were not as popular, and yet many Roman gardens had ponds stocked with freshwater fish.

All of these dishes were cooked in sweet or spicy sauces, and stuffed meats and fish were preferred to those that had been simply boiled or roasted. Many Roman delicacies would seem strange to us today. They put honey in dishes where we would add salt. For seasonings, they often mixed celery, vinegar, raisins, honey, oil, and mint. These were made even more pungent by the addition of a special fermented fish sauce called *garum*.

After the main courses were cleared away, in came the desserts. Many different kinds of honey-sweetened cakes appeared along with fruit. Wine flowed freely and talk would continue long into the night.

**Cicero's Favorite Dish**

*Apicius wrote that Cicero's favorite dish was a sort of goulash made with fish, calves' brains, fowl's liver, hard-boiled eggs, and cheese. This mixture was covered with a pepper sauce that included oregano, wine, honey, oil, raw egg yolks, and caraway seeds.*

## TABLE MANNERS

Influenced by Greek fashion, the Romans adopted the habit of stretching out on a couch at mealtimes. They reclined on their left side with their elbows propped up on cushions. There were three guests on each of the three dining room couches. The place of honor was located to the left of the central couch.

The various dishes were brought to the table precut and sliced into small pieces. Since forks were not yet in use, Romans ate directly from serving platters with their fingers. They used spoons only when eating soups or other liquid specialties. Not surprisingly, dinner guests washed their hands often.

Poor people had dishes made of terracotta, or at the very most, bronze. More fortunate Romans owned fine polished silver. They had plates and shallow bowls as well as wide jugs with narrow necks. Glasses came in a wide variety of sizes and shapes.

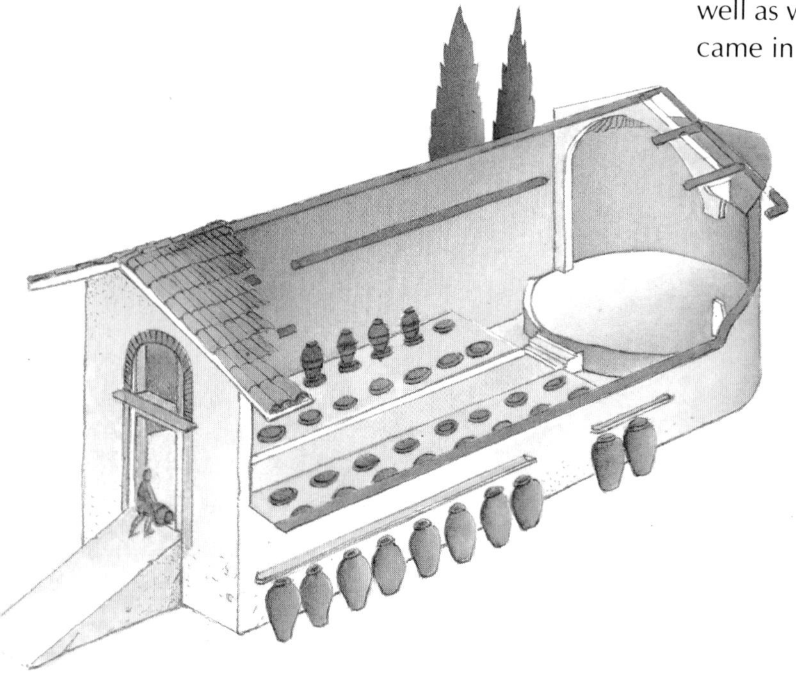

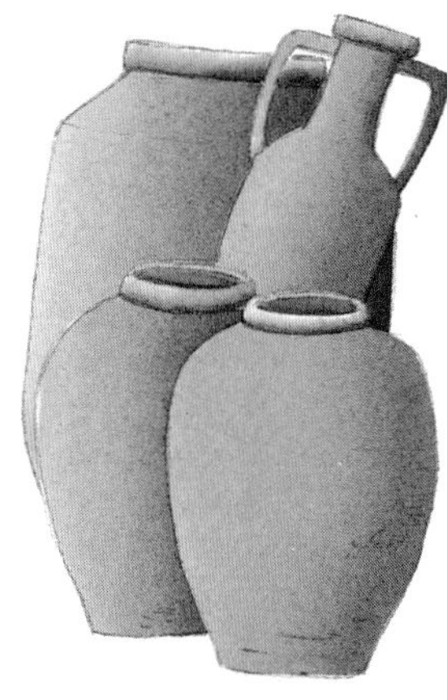

# ENTERTAINMENT

Roman emperors staged many public holidays and sumptuous celebrations as a means of maintaining power. Public parties were a clever way of distracting the Roman people's attention from their loss of republican liberties. The Roman calendar included some 175 national holidays a year!

Important holidays, such as the opening of the Coliseum could last for one hundred consecutive days. Every emperor made it his responsibility to attend the shows and spectacles that were held in the theater, circus, or amphitheater. During intermission, they distributed gifts, surprises, candy, or money to the crowds.

Juvenal criticized the Roman people for caring about only two things in life: bread (*panem*) and the circus (*circens*).

## THEATER

During the Empire, there were three theaters in the city of Rome. During this period, however, the great comedies of Plautus and Terence or the famous tragedies were rarely staged. The general public was much more interested in vulgar spectacles, such as the Atellanes, which included farcical characters reminiscent of Punchinello, Harlequin, and Pierrot.

Very popular mimes and pantomimes were nothing more than parodies of mythological legends. Silent dances where feelings were conveyed through gestures and exaggerated facial expressions were another common form of entertainment.

## BETTING AT THE RACES

The great Roman Circus Maximus was 2,000 feet (610 meters) long, 650 feet (198 meters) wide, and could seat roughly 250,000 spectators. Many popular spectacles such as fights, track racing, trick riding, and chariot races were held at the circus, or arena.

The games' ceremonies always began with a procession in which priests, magistrates, and the competing chariot drivers paraded around the circus. Once the president had signaled the beginning of the games by dropping a handkerchief into the arena, the gates burst open and the four rivals dashed out onto the

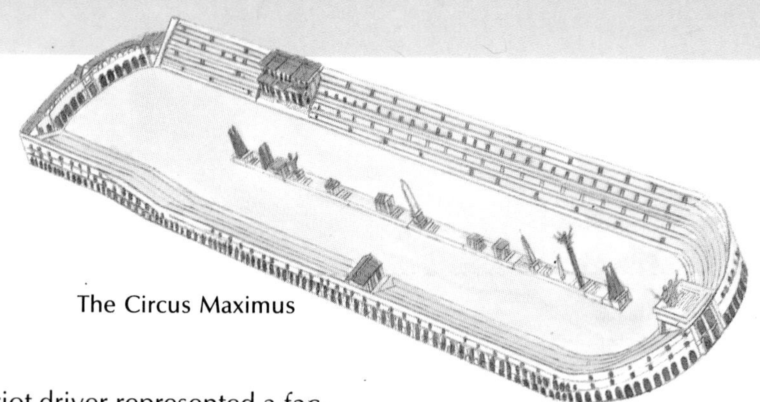
The Circus Maximus

track. Each chariot driver represented a faction, or team. He could be identified by the color of his helmet, which was either blue, green, white, or red.

On the *spina,* the central barrier of the track, stood statues of the gods and seven

wooden eggs, which were gradually replaced by seven bronze dolphins. The changing of these objects allowed spectators to count how many of the seven laps had been run. Roman people got very excited at the races because most of them placed bets on who would win. The green team was always favored by the emperor and the common people, the blues were supported by the Senate and the aristocracy, while those who were opposed to the political regime supported the red and the white teams.

## IN THE AMPHITHEATER

The amphitheater was first and foremost the place where gladiators confronted each other. But other violent, popular spectator sports were also held in the amphitheater.

For example, it was in the amphitheater that the animal fighters, or *bestiarii,* fought wild beasts from Africa. These ferocious animals were sometimes put into the arena to attack helpless criminals, who were chained to posts. It was a cruel and bloody scene. Fights where different kinds of animals were pitted against each other were also well attended. Rhinoceroses fought elephants, bears battled bulls. Even hunting

expeditions were enacted in the amphitheater complete with exotic sets. In the year A.D. 80 during the reign of Titus, roughly 9,000 animals were massacred for the purposes of entertainment. Another 11,000 were killed under Trajan when he celebrated his victory over the Dacians.

The amphitheater was also the site of popular "sea battles." The arena was filled with water so that gladiators could engage in naval combat in small ships.

> **Mirmillones**
>
> *The Gauls were nicknamed the mirmillones because the fish insignia that Gallic gladiators wore on the top of their helmets was a murma (a type of goldfish).*

## GLADIATORS

Gladiators, who underwent special training before making an appearance in the arena, were criminals on death row, prisoners of war, or slaves. Before engaging in combat, gladiators coming into the arena marched before the imperial box and shouted the famous phrase, "Hail Caesar! We who are about to die salute you!"

Gladiators confronted each other one on one. To spice up the spectacle and make the challenge more interesting, each opponent carried a different weapon. Samnites always wore helmets, carried swords and oblong shields, and wore leg armor below the knee. The *retiarii,* or netmen, wore short belted tunics and were equipped with a net to catch their opponent and a trident to stab him. They protected themselves by wearing a metal arm band fitted with a small winged shield that covered the top of the arm and shoulder. The Gauls, whom the Romans called *mirmillones,* wore small helmets decorated with a fish, and carried a small shield and sword. The Thracians were armed with round shields, helmets, leg armor, arm bands, and a short, curved saber.

Gladiators also fought on horseback or in chariots. These horsemen, or *essedarii,* fought from chariots and circled wildly around the center of the arena.

Combatants who had fallen to the ground demanded mercy by lifting their left hand toward the official rostrum. If the chief organizer gave a thumbs down signal, the fighter was killed instantly. If he gave thumbs up, the gladiator was spared.

# ARTS AND SCIENCES

Early Roman peasants did not bother to measure the passage of time. They simply observed the changing seasons, the blossoming of fruit trees, and the course of the moon in the sky. Daily life followed the rhythm of work, meals, and relaxation punctuated by religious holidays.

## MEASURING TIME

The first sundial in Rome was not installed before 164 B.C. The Greek clepsydra, or water clock, was not used until the end of the Republic. Clepsydras could not tell the time of day, but they could be used to measure a given period of time, such as the length of a speech or the amount of time spent at work or play.

When the Republic was proclaimed in 509 B.C., magistrates were elected for twelve-month periods. Their names were written on stone tablets called *fastes,* which served as calendars. The year was named after the two consuls currently holding office. In addition, a nail to mark the year was pounded into the inner wall of the Jupiter temple on the Capitoline Hill. The total nail count allowed Romans to count the number of years that had passed since the founding of the Republic. Since it was known that the kings had ruled for 245 years, Romans were able to determine the dates of important events by counting the years following the birth of Rome in 753 B.C.

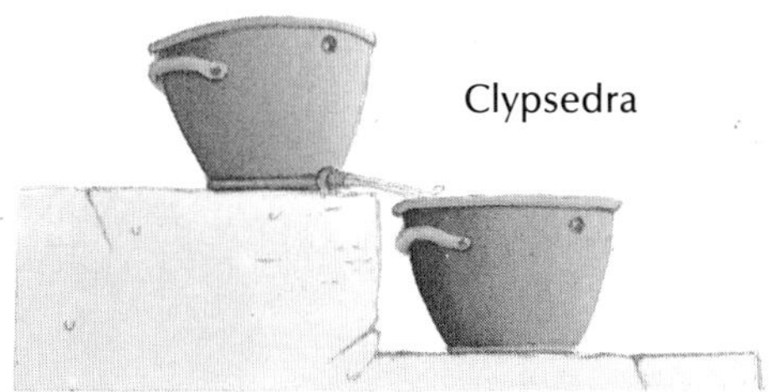

Clypsedra

### *The Roman Calendar*

In 46 B.C., Julius Caesar instituted the 365-day calendar, which included an extra "leap" day every fourth year. During leap year, the Roman calendar included two consecutive February 24ths. The calendars we use today were designed by Caesar and later reformed in 1582 by Pope Gregory XIII.

*Monday, Tuesday, Wednesday*

Romans did not have a seven-day week like ours. Instead, their months were divided into three unequal parts. Three recurring markers allowed them to keep track of the periods within a given month. The calends were always the first day of the

month. The nones marked the fifth day in all months except March, May, July, and October, when it marked the seventh day. The ides fell on the thirteenth day of the month, except in March, May, July, and October, when they came on the fifteenth. The Ides of March came to have a special meaning in ancient Rome. On March 15, 44 B.C., Brutus assassinated Julius Caesar in the Senate. From that day on, the Ides of March was known as an *ater dies*—a black day—thought to bring bad luck.

Other days of the month could be calculated by counting backward from the upcoming marker. For example, Romans regarded the 25th of January as the 8th day before the calends of February, just as in leap year they called the two February 24ths the calends of March.

**Hours**

*Roman days were divided into twelve daylight hours, which lasted from sunrise to sunset, and twelve hours of night. This meant that the length of the hour varied from season to season.*

*Holidays*

On days of the year devoted to religious holidays, neither the tribunes nor the assemblies gathered to carry out the business of the government. Such days were called *nefasti* in contrast to *fasti* days when business went on as usual. A day of rest, or *nundinae,* came every ninth day when townspeople went to market or to visit family and friends. This calendar system meant that Romans had an eight day work week!

## MEDICINE AND MAGIC

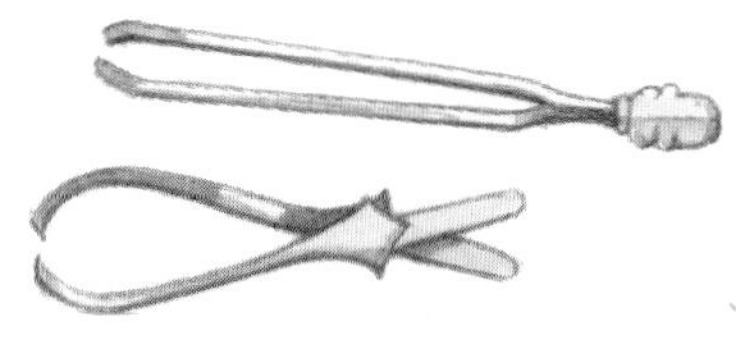

The goal of education was two-fold: students were to cultivate the mind and spirit and develop and maintain good physical health. The long military campaigns against Rome's enemies demanded that the legionnaires be strong and fit. However, hygiene was not good in Roman times; epidemics struck often. To guard their health and bring about a rapid recovery from illness, the Romans called on everyone from doctors and the gods to healers, who were often frauds or quacks.

The temple of Aesculapius on Tiber Island

### *Healing Gods*

A cult formed around Apollo, the god of sunlight, in 431 B.C., after a terrible epidemic. The most important healing god, however, remained Aesculapius who had been the Greek god of healing. A temple built in his honor was erected on Tiber Island in 291 B.C. Here, sick persons underwent a ritual "incubation." While they slept during the night, Aesculapius was supposed to appear to them in a dream and explain what kind of treatment was necessary for them to recover.

### *Doctors*

Like Aesculapius, doctors and medical knowledge came from Greece.

The first of the Roman doctors, mentioned by Pliny the Elder in his work *Nat-*

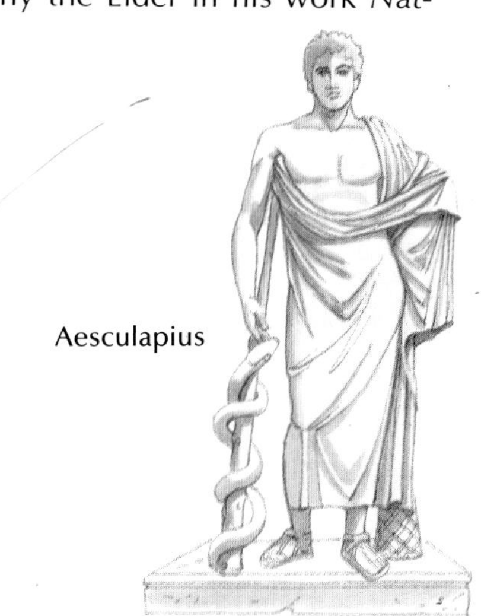

Aesculapius

*ural History,* was a Spartan named Archagathos who settled in Rome in 219 B.C.

Little by little doctors opened practices and clinics and began making house calls and rounds. Many of these early doctors were either freedmen or slaves.

The most well-known doctors quickly found fortune in imperial Rome. In 46 B.C., Caesar granted citizenship to all foreigners practicing medicine in Rome. Hadrian exempted doctors, as well as professors of rhetoric and philosophy, from paying heavy taxes. Doctor Galen, who became the personal physician of Marcus Aurelius, received a large sum of money for healing the wife of an important consul. He was also the preferred physician and surgeon of the gladiators. Galen left a medical encyclopedia that was much admired until the Renaissance in sixteenth-century Europe.

Pharmacists

**Eye Specialists**

*The Romans developed a wide variety of lotions to treat eye infections. The names of these remedies and a list of ingredients were written on the containers so that patients knew what the eye doctor was giving them.*

*Magic*

Despite progress in medical science, the Romans never stopped believing in the power of magical practices and formulas for the treatment of sick patients. For example, in the second century B.C., Cato proposed treating a dislocation in the following way: "Pick a four- or five-foot green reed and break it in half. Two men should each take a half and hold it at their side while repeating the phrase 'motas uaeta daries dardares astataries dissuna piter,' until the two parts of the dislocated limb come back together. Each day recite this incantation 'haut haut haut istasis tarsis ardannabon dannaustra.' " These magic formulas certainly did not make any more sense than our well-known exclamation "abracadabra!" But at a time when little was known about how bones mended or viruses spread, many educated people believed firmly in their power.

## ART LOVERS

During their conquests, Romans, great lovers of music and art, carried many works of art back to Rome to hang in their temples and public places. The city of Rome also attracted a large number of Greek artists.

*Frescoes*

The oldest fresco, or painting on plaster, ever discovered in Rome shows an episode from the Samnite wars (fought between Latium and the region to the southeast called Samnium) and dates back to the third century B.C.

Before a fresco could be painted, the walls had to be covered with three layers of coarse plaster and three layers of a special coating. Colors that were applied while the top coat was still damp were able to stand the test of time.

Canvases showing battle scenes were on public display in the temples and on public buildings. These large paintings were sometimes brought out to celebrate important military victories. Unfortunately, we have only been able to read about these works of art; all of them have disappeared.

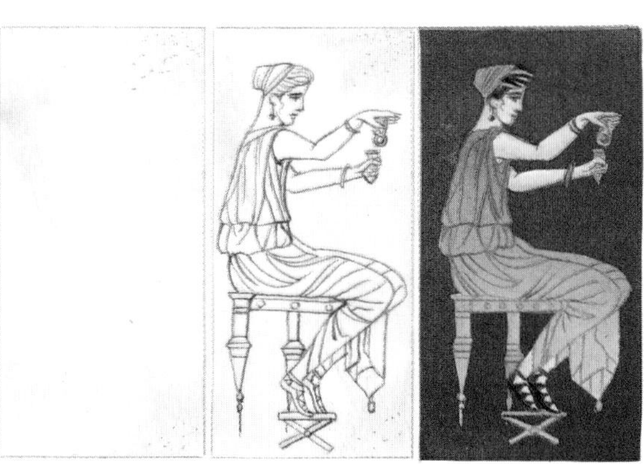

*Murals*

Early Roman decorations were nothing more than imitations of color and reflections of light on marble. Later, artists began to draw buildings, represent perspectives offered by colonnades and roof-lines, and draw countrysides. They painted seaports, rivers, fresh running water, wooded groves, and mountains. They also began to paint mythological scenes illustrating the mythological feats of Hercules, Achilles, Ulysses, and Theseus.

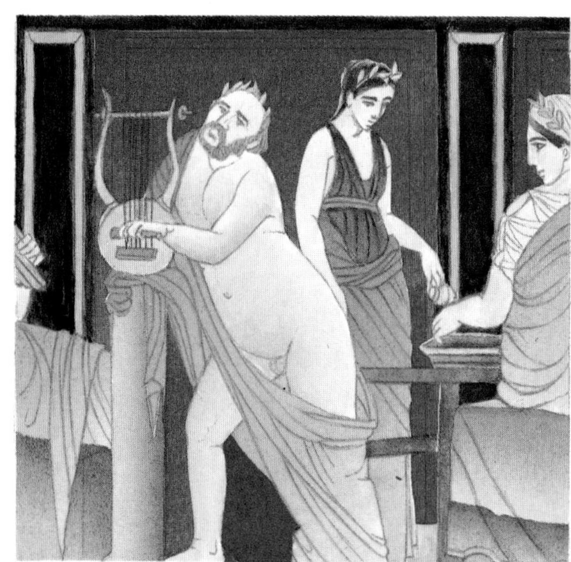

*Sculpture*

Drawing inspiration from Greek art, Romans assigned human characteristics to their gods. But Roman sculptors managed to express their originality through numerous realistic busts of famous men. As for bas-

**Strange Instruments**

*The* scabellum, *which served to keep time, was foot activated and resembled a modern day accordion. The most impressive instrument, however, was a water organ made in Alexandria. This instrument was played at the circus and in the amphitheaters.*

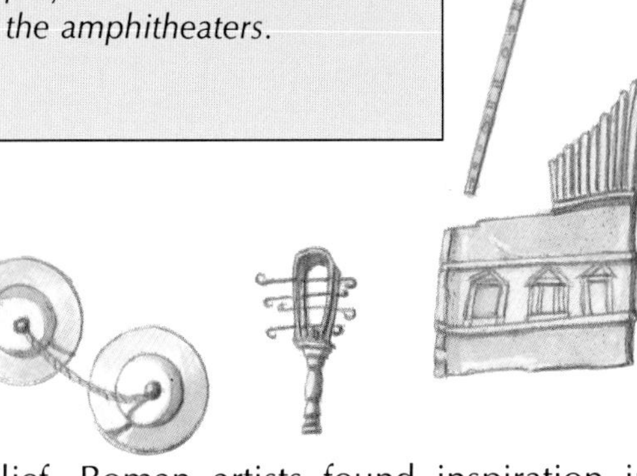

relief, Roman artists found inspiration in urban, military, and religious life. For example, the bas-reliefs that appear on the 200-meter spiral on Trajan's column portray Trajan's two campaigns against the Dacians (101–102 and 105–106).

*Music*

The Romans loved music. They even had a god—Apollo—who was both the sun god and the patron of music. He was often shown in frescoes and bas-reliefs holding a lyre, a stringed instrument from Greece.

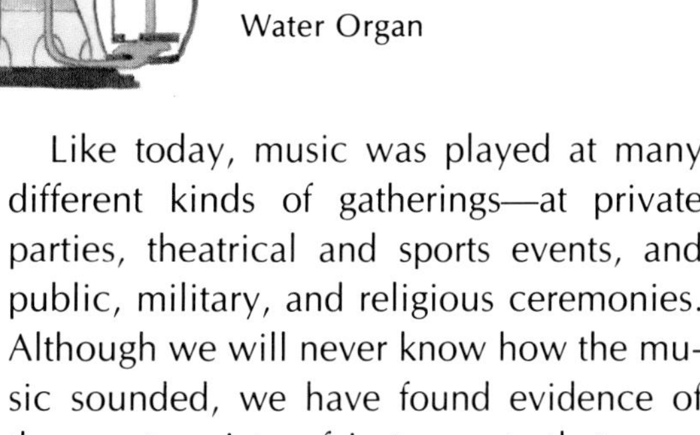

Water Organ

Like today, music was played at many different kinds of gatherings—at private parties, theatrical and sports events, and public, military, and religious ceremonies. Although we will never know how the music sounded, we have found evidence of the great variety of instruments that were played.

In the temples, prayers and sacrifices were accompanied by the sound of double pipes. Special military musicians traveled with the legions and played infantry trumpets *(tubae)* and cavalry trumpets *(lituūs)*. Their spiral horns *(bucinae)* announced the daily routines of military life.

The sounds of quieter musical instruments were heard in the background of banquets, poetry readings, and plays. The airy strains of reed flutes and the gentle plucking of the lyre's strings were common. Horns, winds, and strings might combine in a concert given in a covered theater called an *odeum*.

## LATIN—A DEAD LANGUAGE

At the end of its very long history, Latin gave birth to the romance languages—French, Italian, Spanish, Portuguese, and Rumanian. The history of Latin can be traced from 600 B.C. all the way through to the Middle Ages.

Even when Latin was no longer spoken, it remained the language of scholars, philosophers, and the Church. In the seventeenth century, one of the most important works by the French philosopher René Descartes, *Meditations on Metaphysics,* was written in Latin. Many eighteenth-century philosophers continued to write in Latin. Very few languages throughout the history of the world have had such a long history.

Latin became a dead language when it stopped being understood by the people to whom priests were addressing their sermons and when it came to be replaced by national languages. All living languages evolve. The language we speak today will undoubtedly be difficult for our descendants in the twenty-second century to understand.

### *Languages of Antiquity*

Latin was at the root of the language spoken by the people living in Latium and the lower Tiber valley. The Roman conquests fostered the spread of this language throughout Italy and eventually all the lands surrounding the Mediterranean basin. Other similar dialects were spoken by the neighboring peoples of Rome. Umbrian, for example, was spoken in central Italy, and Oscan was spoken in the south. Greek was the language of the colonies founded by Greeks in the south, and Gaulois, a Celtic language, was spoken by Gauls in the north. All of these languages belong to the same Indo-European language family.

However, in the hilly region of northwestern Italy known today as Tuscany, the Etruscans, whose origins remain unknown, had developed a brilliant and highly structured civilization as early as the sixth cen-

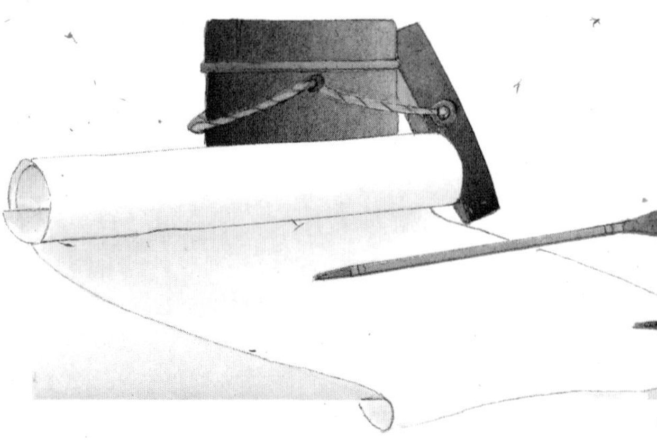

**The Pin at Palestrina:**

*Beautiful pins, or small jewels designed to decorate and fasten clothing, were made of gold and some carried inscriptions. On the pin (fibula) at Palestrina, reading from right to left, it says: Manios med fhefhaked Numasioi ("Manius made me for Numerius"). The pin spoke in the first person. Manius was the name of the man who made or gave the jewel. Numerius was the person who received it. In ancient culture, gift-giving played an important role.*

tury B.C. Although we have learned many things about their society through the thousands of sculptures and artifacts dug out of their elaborate cemeteries, their unique language remains an unsolvable mystery to us today.

*Oldest Traces of Latin*

The first Indo-Europeans arrived in Italy about 1000 B.C. Rome was founded in 753 B.C. The oldest-known Latin inscription dates back to about 600 B.C. It was inscribed on a gold pin, or *fibula*, found in a tomb at Palestrina in central Italy. In 1899, another archaic inscription was discovered. The *Lapis Niger*, or black stone, makes mention of an old religious law dating back to roughly 500 B.C.

Latin literature began to develop much later. In the third century B.C., writers began to find inspiration in works written in Greek. Many Greek plays were translated into Latin. The basic forms were imitated, while the subjects were changed to reflect Roman concerns. Even historians such as Cato and Sallust based their writings on Greek models.

Ancient Rome also nourished many writers whose expression was entirely original. Beautiful poetry was written. The works of Catullus, Lucretius, Ovid, and Virgil have served as models to many poets of the European tradition. And the brilliance of the historian Tacitus continues to be studied with much interest to this day. Other great Roman works include the speeches and letters of Cicero and the humorous satires of Horace and Juvenal.

# ROMAN GODS

Religious life centered around the temple, which Romans regarded as a sacred and holy place. However, other sites were also regarded as sacred: the entire city of Rome, military camps, and even some colonies.

Deities—gods and goddesses, demigods (half-human and half-god), and spirits—were found everywhere throughout the natural world. Nevertheless, the gods were symbolized by statues that represented their human forms. The principal gods were usually shown to be oversized humans. They were easy to recognize

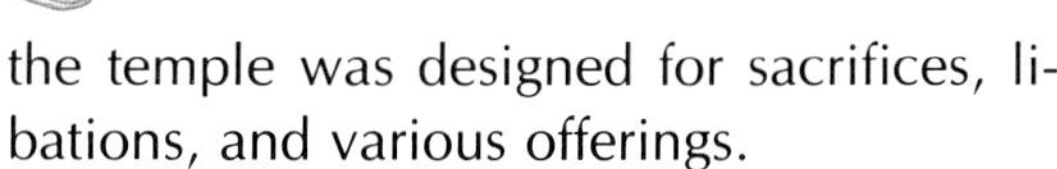

because the depictions of the gods did not vary much. Jupiter, the king of gods, reigned in the sky. His symbols were the eagle and the thunderbolt. His wife, Juno, the patron goddess of women, often appeared with a peacock. Minerva, goddess of war, had a helmet and armor, while the messenger of the gods, Mercury, wore wings.

Temples were the homes that Romans created for their gods. The god's statue was kept deep within the temple, which stood on top of a heavy foundation and was surrounded by colonnades. A flight of odd-numbered stairs led to the entrance of the temple.

Only priests serving the deity were allowed inside the temple. Worshipers had to remain outside. An altar table outside the temple was designed for sacrifices, libations, and various offerings.

Temples sometimes included several adjoining buildings, which resulted in very large sanctuaries, or places of worship. For example, hidden in the base of the Temple of Saturn was an enormous state treasure. In the base of the Aesculapian temple, dormitories housed the faithful. Believers brought gifts to the temple (either elaborate presents or a simple offering), to thank the gods for their help during times of stress, war, or illness.

### *Sacred Statues*

The statue of the god stood in the temple's shadowy darkness. The priests prayed to the statue or covered it with precious un-

guents or perfumes. Only on very rare occasions, such as extreme danger or great military victory, was the statue brought outside to the temple's vestibule. Crowds bowed low before the sacred artifact.

Once in a while, gods would participate in sacred banquets. The statue of the god was laid on a couch surrounded with offerings. This important ritual was called *lectisterne*.

*Other Religious Sites*

The *lararium,* or *sacrarium,* was a small chapel found in the atrium of every Roman home. The atrium contained an altar and hearth where the sacred flame burned. In addition, niches or cupboards protected small wax statues representing the gods of the family hearth *(lar familiaris)* who guarded over the house, and the *Penatium,* gods of the household who looked after the well-being of the family.

**Primitive Temples**

*Most temples were rectangular, but some were circular. For example, the temple of Vesta, which sheltered the city's sacred flame, was circular like the primitive dwellings of early Romans.*

Deities were also thought to live in sacred woods and around fountains. Along roadsides and passageways, travelers often came across little chapels with a statue of a god as well as altars for offerings and sacrifices.

## RELIGIOUS LIFE

The Romans' religious spirit was a practical one. For example, for each agricultural task, there was a specific god to whom the peasant could turn for help. Sentiment and faith were much less important than the careful way in which the sacred acts were performed.

The Ponifex Maximus, who sat at the head of the College of Pontiffs, was respon-

Minerva

sible for organizing the religious calendar and deciding which days would be reserved for the gods as *dies nefasti* and which were to be *dies fasti* devoted to the routine activities of work and play.

Ritual prayers, rules for sacrifices, and the running of games were recorded in the pontifical books. All the military and political events of the city were also noted in the pontifical annals, which were much like a diary of Rome.

### *Roman Prayer*

Romans prayed silently to their gods with their arms stretched out in front of them. They stood facing the direction of the rising sun and covered their heads with a veil or a fold of their toga.

In the privacy of their homes, Roman worshipers were allowed to touch the altar or even kiss the statue of the god to whom they were speaking. Worshipers sometimes blew kisses at the gods as a gesture of adoration.

Public prayers involved many specific precautions. An assistant read the phrase to be recited by the priest, while another helper checked that all the terms to be used were correct. A flute player accompanied the recitation and ensured that no other sounds interfered with the ceremony. The slightest hesitation or stammering would destroy the prayer's effect.

### *Sacrificial Animals*

Cattle, pigs, and sheep were selected as sacrificial animals. The animal to be slaughtered had to be free of any physical defect. Sacred servants led the animal to the altar. During this part of the ritual, it was important that the animal make no attempt to escape. After the priest had granted permission, the animal was felled with an ax or mallet. Another assistant cut its throat with a knife so that blood would run over the altar. The priest examined the animal's inner organs before burning them to make sure that the gods were satisfied. The animal's meat was shared among the priests and assistants. The sacrifice served as a common meal that united the gods and men.

Romans were anxious to maintain good relationships with their gods. For this reason, they were careful to observe all religious rites and obligations. They believed that the gods showed their unhappiness with human beings by sending signs such as earthquakes, hailstorms, and other mysterious occurrences. The sacred college interpreted such celestial signs as the flight and sound of song birds and the roar of thunder.

*From Many Gods to One*

Romans inherited many of their gods from the Greeks. They also prayed to gods from other countries, such as the Egyptian gods Isis and Serapis, who symbolized the cycle of life, death, and rebirth; the Middle Eastern mother goddess Cybele; and Mithras, a Persian god who was thought to have created life, and who was worshiped only by men.

Christianity was the only religion that the Romans would not tolerate. But this did not stem the flow of belief in a single god, which by the end of the first century had spread throughout Asia Minor and was beginning to spill over into the west.

Within several hundred years, Christians came to outnumber pagans, or people who believed in many gods. The ascent of Christianity coincided with the decline of the Roman Empire. "Barbarians" invaded from the north, and civil war raged within. The giant structure sagged under the weight of corruption and economic burdens. This fertile empire eventually came to an end. But the wealth of expression born out of Roman civilization has not stopped enriching our lives to this day.

**Vestal Virgins**

*The goddess of fire, Vesta, symbolized Rome's sacred flame, which was never to be extinguished. The flame was kept in Vesta's circular temple and guarded by the Vestal Virgins. These women were chosen as young girls from among Rome's great families. After pronouncing a vow of purity, they devoted themselves to the worship of the goddess for a period of thirty years.*

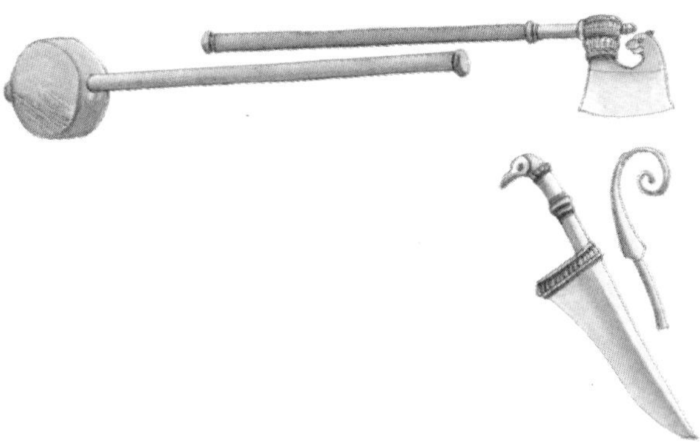

# DATES TO REMEMBER

753 B.C. Birth of Rome

753–509 Royal Dynasty

509 Establishment of the Republic

450 Laws of the Twelve Tables

264–241 First Punic War (Rome against Carthage)

218–201 Second Punic War

168 Romans defeat the King of Macedonia at Pydna

146 Destruction of Carthage

82–79 Sulla's Dictatorship

59 Julius Caesar as Consul

58–51 The Gallic War

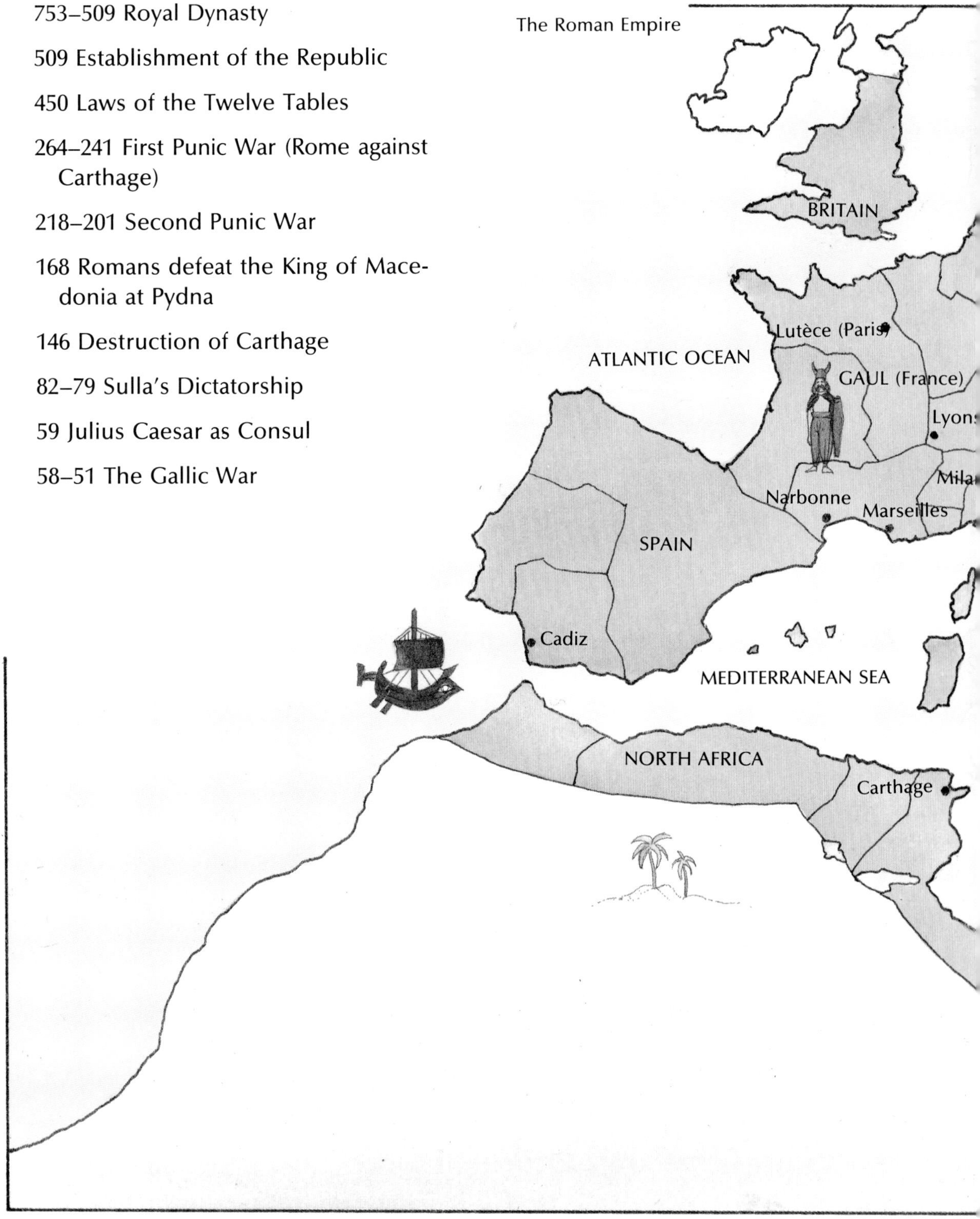

The Roman Empire

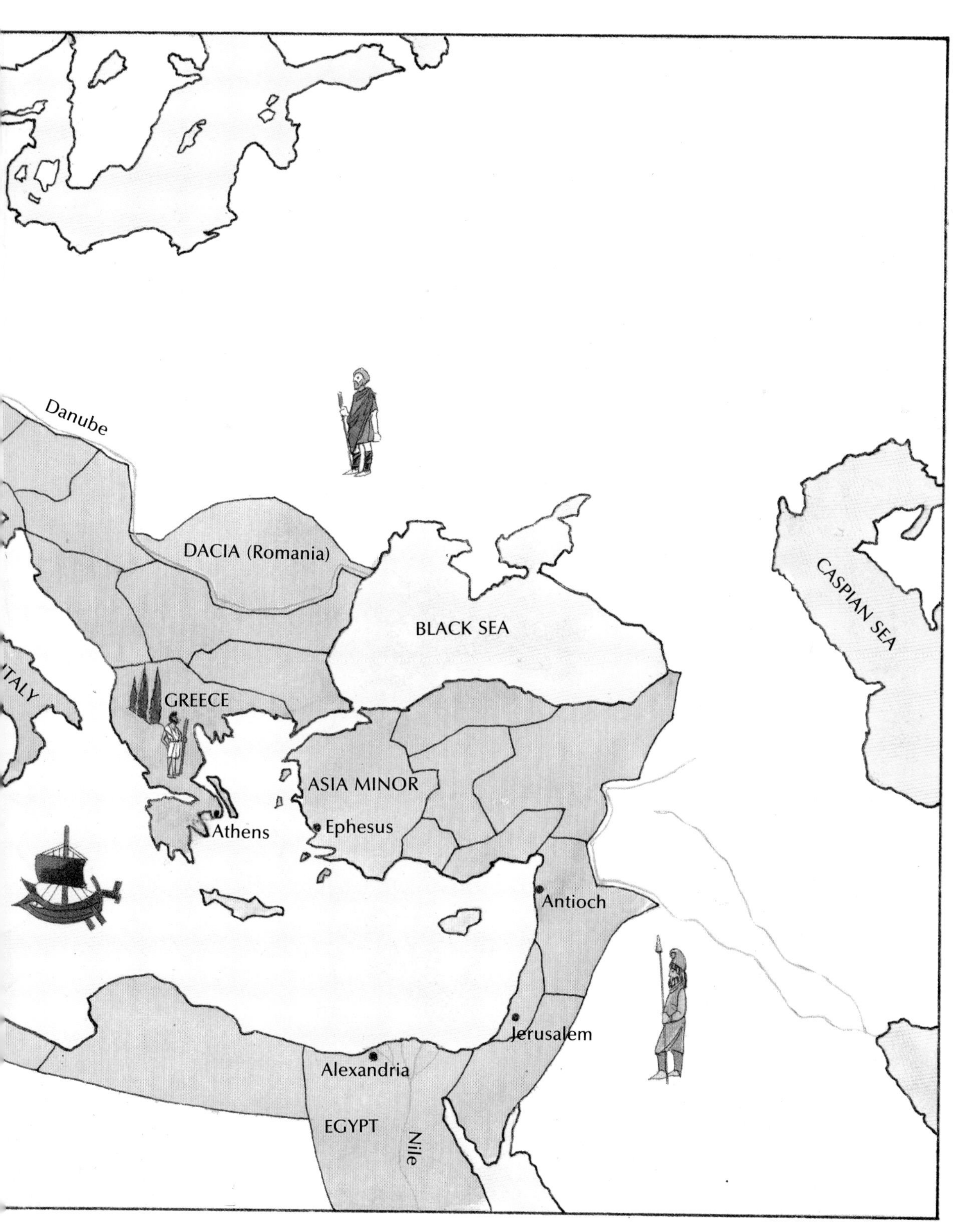

Danube
DACIA (Romania)
BLACK SEA
CASPIAN SEA
TALY
GREECE
ASIA MINOR
Athens
Ephesus
Antioch
Jerusalem
Alexandria
EGYPT
Nile

# DATES TO REMEMBER (continued)

49 Caesar crosses the Rubicon (and drives Pompeii out of Rome)

44 Death of Caesar (Caesar is assassinated by Brutus)

31 Battle of Actium; Octavian (Augustus) is victorious

27 The Republic ends; the Roman Empire is born

14 A.D. Death of Augustus

14–68 Julio-Claudian Dynasty

53–117 Reign of Trajan

117–138 Reign of Hadrian

161–180 Reign of Marcus Aurelius

212 Caracalla grants all free men the right to establish residence in the Empire

313 By the Edict of Milan, Constantine decrees religious liberty

337 Death of Constantine

395 The Empire is divided (between the two sons of Theodosius the Great)

410 Sack of Rome by Alaric, King of the Visigoths

451 Attila moves into Gaul

455–476 The last Western Roman emperors

476 End of the Western Roman Empire

# FIND OUT MORE ABOUT THE ROMANS

*Ancient Rome* by John Altman (Carthage, IL: Good Apple, 1991).

*Ancient Rome* by Keith Brandt (Mahwah, NJ: Troll, 1985).

*Living in Ancient Rome* by Odile Bombarde and Claude Moatti (Ossining, NY: Young Discovery Library, 1988).

*Living in Roman Times* by Jan Chisholm (Tulsa, OK: EDC Publishing, 1982).

*The Roman Army* by John Wilkes (Minneapolis, MN: Lerner Publications, 1977).

*Roman Forts* by Margaret Mulvihill (NY: Watts, 1986).

*The Romans* by Pamela Odijk (Englewood Cliffs, NJ: Silver Burdett, 1989).

*Rome* by Simon James (NY: Watts, 1987).

*See Inside a Roman Town* by Jonathan Rutland (NY: Watts, 1986).

# GLOSSARY

**Amphitheater.** A circular stadium for spectacles and contests, with tiered seats around an open space.

**Aqueduct.** A trough used to carry large quantities of water.

**Arena.** The open space in an amphitheater where spectacles took place.

**Atrium.** A rectangular open courtyard around which Roman houses were built.

**Basilica.** The building where the judicial and commercial activities of the city took place.

**Bas-relief.** A sculpture carved in a flat stone or marble surface.

**Calends.** The first day of the month according to the Roman calendar.

**Catapult.** A large slingshot-like device used to hurl stones and heavy objects at enemy cities.

**Century.** A division of one hundred Roman soldiers in a Roman legion.

**Cohort.** A troop of soldiers or civil servants.

**Consul.** One of the two men who were elected by the people to assume joint leadership of the Republic.

**Crepundia.** A noisemaker and good luck charm.

**Dies fasti.** Work days.

**Dies nefasti.** Religious holidays.

**Dome.** A round vault on a circular base.

**Empire.** The form of government in which the emperor had supreme authority. The Roman Empire began with the rule of Augustus in 27 B.C. and continued until the end of the Western Roman Empire in A.D. 476. The Eastern Roman, or Byzantine, Empire survived until 1453.

**Equites.** A landowner or wealthy businessman.

**Fastes.** A stone tablet on which the names of the Roman magistrates were written.

**Forum.** The center of Roman cities, where the market, government, and religious buildings were found.

**Gladiator.** Trained fighters, often slaves or criminals, who engaged in combat in Roman amphitheaters.

**Honestiories.** Upper-class Romans.

**Humiliores.** Craftsmen and shop owners.

**Ides.** The thirteenth or fifteenth day of the month according to the Roman calendar.

**Insula.** The name for an apartment house.

**Lararium.** A small chapel found in a Roman house.

**Legate.** The general in command of the Roman legions.

**Legion.** The largest unit in the Roman military, averaging 6,000 men at the height of the Empire.

**Maniple.** A division of 60 or 120 Roman soldiers in a Roman legion.

**Nones.** The fifth or seventh day of the month according to the Roman calendar.

**Odeum.** A covered theater.

**Pagan.** A person who, like the Romans, worships many different gods.

**Palaestra.** A school for sports such as wrestling.

**Pax Romana.** (Roman Peace). The period of stability in the Roman Empire, beginning with the rule of Augustus in 27 B.C. and ending with the death of Marcus Aurelius in A.D. 180.

**Penates.** A Roman household god who secured the well-being of the family.

**Republic.** The form of government from 509 to 27 B.C., in which a body of Roman citizens ruled.

**Senate.** The group of men who advised the king in the period before the Republic, the consuls during the Republic, and the emperor during the Roman Empire.

**Stola.** A woman's pleated robe, worn over a tunic.

**Sudarium.** A Roman steam bath.

**Toga.** Draped material worn over a tunic.

**Tunic.** The most commonly worn garment in ancient Rome, made from two rectangles of cloth sewn together.

**Vault.** An arched masonry structure.

**Vestal virgin.** A woman who guarded Rome's sacred flame.

# INDEX